THE AWAKENING OF HUMANITY

BENJAMIN CREME

Share International Foundation
Amsterdam • London

Manufactured in the United States on recycled paper

First Edition, June 2008

*The picture reproduced on the cover – **Flame-coloured Deva** – was painted by Benjamin Creme between 1976 and 1977. The Deva or Angelic evolutions are parallel to that of the human and of infinite variety and colour, from subhuman to superhuman. Many work in a direct healing and protective relation to humanity.*

This book is dedicated to my
revered Master Whose inspiration
has made it possible.

TABLE OF CONTENTS

PREFACE

The *Awakening of Humanity* is intended as a companion volume to *The World Teacher for All Humanity*, published in 2007. That book focused on the nature of Maitreya, the World Teacher: His extraordinary capacity to express the qualities of wisdom and love as a great Spiritual Avatar, as well as a friend and brother of us all.

The Awakening of Humanity focuses on the day when Maitreya declares Himself openly as World Teacher for the age of Aquarius. In His article 'To Serve Anew', reprinted in this book, my Master describes movingly the expected reaction of humanity on that day. My commentary on the Master's article follows. Although the Master's article and my commentary were published previously in *Maitreya's Mission, Volume Three*, Chapter 3, we reprint them here in order to draw readers' attention once again to this unprecedented event in human history. The questions and answers that follow relate to the process of Maitreya's emergence and the Day of Declaration, as well as to the themes raised in the Master's article. Most of the questions are taken from past issues of *Share International* magazine and, with a few exceptions, have not been published in previous books.

Readers are encouraged to read 'Maitreya's Priorities', Chapter 1 of *Maitreya's Mission, Volume Three*, for a more detailed discussion of the priorities Maitreya is advocating, as well as the extraordinary nature of His work.

My account of the Day of Declaration is excerpted from my talk in Tokyo in 2007 and is printed below. For a more thorough understanding of the background of this story, please refer to the Overview in *The World Teacher for All Humanity*.

Day of Declaration

When the world stock markets collapse – as soon as it is obvious that they are on their final plunge – Maitreya will emerge. He will take up an invitation to appear on a major television network in the United States. The invitation has already been issued, but Maitreya will determine the timing of the interview. After the initial interview, all the networks will want to interview Him. However, He will not be introduced as Maitreya or the Christ, but simply as a man of extraordinary wisdom and love.

Maitreya does not come as a religious teacher, but as a spiritual teacher. We have to broaden our idea of what 'spiritual' is. We have to spiritualize every aspect of our lives.

The problem is the commercialization of all aspects of life. We say it in two words – market forces. Market forces are the excuse for everything that we do. Maitreya says commercialization is more dangerous to the world than an atomic bomb.

When we share the produce of the world more equitably, we at a stroke make war and terrorism a thing of the past. We create the conditions of trust. When we have trust, we can sit down and work out the answer to every problem.

Thus will Maitreya speak. Look for such a man speaking in those terms, much more eloquently and simply than I have done. If you believe that He is speaking truly, make it your work to be the first to change, the first to sacrifice.

When enough people are following, not Maitreya, but the thoughts, the ideas, the advice of Maitreya, He will be invited to speak to the entire world on what we will call the Day of Declaration. On that day Maitreya will appear on the television sets of everyone at the same time throughout the world. He will address the world, but will not actually speak.

Maitreya is omniscient and omnipresent, and will create during this time a telepathic rapport with every adult in the world. Everyone will hear Maitreya's thoughts, His ideas, His hopes, His plans for the future, telepathically, inwardly in their own language. The Japanese will hear Him in Japanese, the French in French, the Germans in German, the Chinese in Chinese, and so on. He will tell humanity about itself, about how old we are, how long we have been evolving to this relative point (not so high as we think). He will show what lies ahead, the science of the future.

Maitreya will show the high level from which we have fallen, into the mediocrity of materialism today. And He will show the way forward, through the acceptance of the principle of sharing, declaring our sense of the one brotherhood and sisterhood of humanity, enabling us to set out again on the spiritual path, the path that leads not to competition but to oneness.

That is what the New Age is about, the Age of Synthesis. Synthesis means the drawing together and creation of oneness, a unity out of disparate parts. You will find that is the aim of the evolutionary process: unity in diversity, the greatest diversity in the fullness of unity.

While He is speaking, Maitreya's energy will flow out in tremendous potency through the hearts of all humanity. This will evoke an intuitive, heartfelt response to the message. On the physical plane there will be hundreds of thousands of spontaneous miracle healings throughout the world. In these three ways you will know that that One and, of course, only that One, is Maitreya Buddha, the Christ, the Imam Mahdi, Kalki Avatar, Krishna, Messiah, by whatever name He is looked for and awaited. That day will define the entire future for humanity.

Benjamin Creme
London, March 2008

"Soon the world will know of the Splendour in its midst. Soon will men weep for joy at His appearance. Soon, too, will they take upon themselves the task of succour, re-establishing the true unity of men. Thus will it be."

(From the article, 'The Great Lord emerges' by the Master –)

TO SERVE ANEW

by the Master –, through Benjamin Creme*

Since the time is short indeed till mankind sees the Christ, it would be wise to consider, somewhat, the likely repercussions of that momentous event. Firstly, men will awaken to a new situation, one altogether unfamiliar and strange: nothing similar will have been the experience of anyone alive; no one, anywhere, will have heard before the thoughts broadcast on that day of days. Never, before, will men have heard the call to their divinity, the challenge to their presence here on Earth. Each, singly, and solemnly alone, will know for that time the purpose and meaning of their lives, will experience anew the grace of childhood, the purity of aspiration cleansed of self. For these precious minutes, men will know afresh the joy of full participation in the realities of Life, will feel connected one to another, like the memory of a distant past.

Suddenly, men will realize that their life till now was a shallow thing, lacking, for the majority, all that makes life dear: brotherhood and justice, creativeness and love. Many will know for the first time that they count, that they matter in the scheme of things. An unfamiliar sense of self-esteem will replace their present hopelessness; drugs of all kinds will cease their hold on men. Quietly, men's tears will flow in humble gratitude and longing for the good.

From that time forwards, a new spirit of sanctity will prevail upon the Earth; men will walk on tiptoe for a time. Soon, however, men will realize that the changes needed in the world are vast, manifold, requiring patience and dedication, imagination and trust. Before long, men everywhere will engage themselves in the work of reconstruction, the rehabilitation of the world. Succour for the poor and hungry will take pride of place, and so will end for ever a blasphemy in men's midst: millions will know for the first time the quiet happiness of satisfied need – no more will the dying forms of the starving disgrace the screens of the affluent; no longer will men watch their brothers dying before their eyes. So will end a dark chapter in the history of the race.

Changes, unequalled in extent, will engage men's minds and hearts; naught but the finest of the past will prevail against the onslaught of the new. Daily, the transformations will be recorded for men to compare and admire; a new world will be constructed in the blazing light of day. All will, in their way, participate, each will add his vision and contribute to the whole.

For many, the very presence of the Christ will constitute a problem – their long-held beliefs will be shaken to their core. For them, a period of heart searching will be inevitable as they seek to understand the meaning of the new dispensation; ancient beliefs die hard and hurt bitterly in the process. Nevertheless, millions will respond with a glad heart, happy to accept the Teacher in their midst. Few, in time, will stand against the common acknowledgment that the Christ, in the person of Maitreya, walks once more upon the Earth.

Those relatively few who have led the way in preparation for this time will find themselves offered another field of service: an educational endeavour vast in scope. From all sides will come the queries; a long-felt hunger for knowledge will, like a dammed-up river, overflow and burst its banks. Many will seek to know the background and history of this event; for others, the immediate future will be the chief concern. Still others will feel the need to analyse and to question every explanation, unsatisfied in the end with aught but their own beliefs. Persuasion and tact, therefore, must be the order of the day, so to avoid the charge of bigotry and pride.

Societies, worldwide, will play their part, assuring the broad dissemination of the needed teachings. Much remains to be given, but, already, much remains unopened and unread in the hands of men. Endeavour, the counsel is, to inculcate the habit of reading much, thus to inform and guide the seekers on the way. Systematic study of the teachings, and earnest attempts to live the precepts of Maitreya, will give the needed balance and authority with which to teach. Each one, thus equipped, can avail themselves of this opportunity to serve anew. Seize it, the counsel is, with alacrity and humble pride.

A Master Speaks, pg. 274

*This article by Benjamin Creme's Master was first published in *Share International* magazine and later published in the book *A Master Speaks* (third expanded edition, 2004).

THE AWAKENING OF HUMANITY

The following article is an edited version of the talk by Benjamin Creme given during the July 1994 Transmission Meditation Conference in San Francisco, USA.

Kali Yuga

"Firstly, men will awaken to a new situation, one altogether unfamiliar and strange: nothing similar will have been the experience of anyone alive."

I do not know whether you have thought of it, but this is manifestly true. When Maitreya speaks as the World Teacher for the new age, enlightening humanity with certain ideas that, as students of the esoteric tradition, we take for granted and with which we have familiarized ourselves in the process of making known His presence, most people are going to have an extraordinary revelation.

The world as a whole does not know that Hierarchy exists. They have heard that the Christ exists, but living up in heaven in some remote place in the sky – waiting until the end of the world to return on a cloud. That, as you know, is the general expectation of orthodox Christians. The other religions have their equally unlikely scenarios for the coming of the Teacher into our midst. Muslims are awaiting the Imam Mahdi Who, likewise, can only come on Judgment Day, again at the end of the world; and into Damascus, the "centre of the world", at noon, when He will appear suddenly and say: "I have come. Give Me bread. Give Me clothes." Hindus have their own interpretation, awaiting Kalki Avatar or the return of Krishna, at the end of Kali Yuga.

I heard the other day that Sai Baba [a great Avatar based in southern India Who works closely with Maitreya] had announced recently that Kali Yuga had ended, was coming now to an end. I thought that He had said that several years ago, and we published it in *Share International,* but we are always ahead of events! My Master affirmed, as did Swami Premananda, that Kali Yuga was indeed ending and we published that at the same time.

However, there has been a rumour, as always, coming from Puttaparti, that Sai Baba has said that Kali Yuga has now ended, and that this week, from Monday 18 to today Friday 22 July 1994, was a most important period in the life of this Earth. He did not, as far as I know, go on to explain why it was important, why it was so crucial. I have checked up, of course, with my own source of information. Indeed, what Sai Baba appears to have been referring to is that this week is the culmination of a great period of trial and testing for the Earth, and that the Earth has come through it – that is, mainly humanity, although not only humanity – safely.

For example, a great battle has been going on, on cosmic levels, between the forces of Light, under Maitreya, and certain evil cosmic forces. That has culminated recently in a triumph for our Spiritual Hierarchy. Maitreya has been waiting for just such a time to emerge into the open. As you know, at other times, in particular in 1985 when Maitreya was ready to come forward to a group of journalists meeting in London, there was a great battle fought, again on cosmic levels, between these forces and our own planetary Hierarchy. This, too, ended in a triumph for our Hierarchy, but at the expense of the coming forward of Maitreya. It took all the combined efforts of Hierarchy to contain the assault which was launched.

I know the signs. I know that during such a period when cosmic battles are going on, about which humanity hears nothing, my Master becomes very remote indeed. I can sense His remoteness. Although He will respond and will answer questions, it is as if His answers are coming through a series of filters and barriers. All the Masters were totally focused, meditating. The same thing happened in the two or three months before July 1977, when Maitreya came down from His retreat in the Himalayas.

Having accepted the invitation to appear on a major US network, He has been waiting for the best possible moment in which to do it. That would be when the spiritual energies in the world were at their highest, when a reservoir had been built up which would guarantee (as far as that can ever be guaranteed) a correct response from humanity. So that it would not be wasted, that the maximum response of a good kind, positive and welcoming, would come from such a broadcast.

During the Three Spiritual Festivals, in April, May and June, powerful energies were poured into the world – the Spirit of Peace, the Buddha, the Avatar of Synthesis, the energies from Aquarius focused through Maitreya, and so on. All of this has been building up in tremendous potency. The Avatar of Synthesis, in particular, I have experienced as never before, coming also with the Shamballa force, which is unusual; it is usually one or the other. This has built up a barrier against these cosmic forces which have been levelled against us, a last ditch stand, if you like, of these materialistic forces, trying to prevent the manifestation of our Spiritual Hierarchy openly in the world.

They have not succeeded, they will not succeed, and the way is now clear for the open manifestation of Maitreya and the other Masters. I believe that is what Sai Baba meant when He said that the period from 18-22 July will be of major import. It has turned the wheel. We are now in the age of Aquarius. I know Maitreya said that when the Earth was slowed down in its revolution, brought symbolically closer to the sun, that was the turning of the wheel. That was the beginning of a process which has culminated now. We are at the end of Kali Yuga, and at the end of Kali Yuga the Kalki Avatar can come. Maitreya is, of course, the Kalki Avatar.

Even on the Day of Declaration, I doubt very much that Maitreya will say: "I am the Christ." He will probably say

11

something like: "Many millions await Me as the Christ, and it is to fulfil their expectations that I come." Something of that nature.

He will introduce to the world as a whole the fact that He has been living in the Himalayas, rather than in 'heaven', this past 2,000 years and more; that He is the head of a large group of similarly, if not equally, advanced men, and that They too, in growing numbers, will be in the world. Already a large number, 14 including Maitreya, are among us.

This will be a revelation for humanity. There is one thing on which I disagree with the Master DK. I find it very difficult to agree when He says that the idea of Hierarchy has filtered right down to "the man in the street". I would have thought that probably everyone in California today has heard of the Masters. But Kansas City? Cleveland? Detroit? I doubt it. Manchester? Birmingham? Bremen? Yokohama? No, I think that there are many places in the world, most of them in particular, where the idea of Hierarchy has never entered into the consciousness of the people.

Yet they are going to hear about it for the first time on the Day of Declaration. And they are going to hear about it from the One Who knows about it, Who leads the whole group of Masters, and in this miraculous way by their minds being over-shadowed. As the Master put it, "*singly, and solemnly alone*" they will hear this voice in their hearts. Can you imagine the experience this will be for the bulk of humanity, who have never before heard of Masters or a Christ Who isn't up in heaven; a great teacher Who is actually there on a television screen speaking for the first time to the whole of humanity in this extraordinary way? Can you imagine what that will mean, the shock to the consciousness of the vast body of humanity, probably most of the 6.3 billion people who live in the world.

I have never yet grasped the immensity of this event. I have said it so many times, but never until this moment, and probably not at this moment, have I been able to grasp the enormous impact of that, the enormity, the newness, uniqueness, of this event. For the first time in history there will be a world telepathic contact. The whole world will be in contact with one man, hearing His words enter their minds in their own language, speaking directly to them, *"singly, and solemnly alone"*. Every individual will be watching the screen. They will turn to each other to ask: "Are you hearing what I am hearing?" Because of the tone of the voice, as it were, the tone of the thought, the solemnity of the ideas, the vastness of these concepts, people will be experiencing what they have never experienced in their lives. That is phenomenal. We are standing at a unique moment in the history of this planet.

"Altogether unfamiliar." That is the understatement of the year. *"Altogether unfamiliar and strange."* A new situation. Suddenly, people will know that we do not have to wait for UFOs to descend to have enlightened Beings in our midst. We will know that 'that' man is the most enlightened Being we are likely to meet. And He is not alone; He has a large group of similarly enlightened men Who are going to live among us, Who are going to be accessible: to know, to learn from, to guide and advise humanity. That must mean a phenomenal lifting of the weight of anxiety and depression. You can imagine what effect that will have when humanity, living largely in stress and anxiety, hears His words of hope and concern.

Most people, whether they are starving to death or multimillionaires, are living under stress. Anyone living today who is halfway sensitive must be living under conditions of strain, of tension: of inward expectation because of their sensitivity as souls, but perhaps not knowing what is taking place, responding to the energies perhaps negatively, finding them simply an imposition, trying to drive them in directions in which they do not want to go. Others gladly accept these energies, and without knowing that they are there, bring out the constructive ideas which will give form to the experience of the energies. People are going to have these different reactions, not only to the energies, but to the One Who carries these energies, the Water Carrier. Whether He will call Himself the Water Carrier on that day, I do not know. My guess is that He will.

"No one, anywhere, will have heard before the thoughts broadcast on that day of days. Never before will men have heard the call to their divinity, the challenge to their presence here on Earth."

It is a challenge. Maitreya will present to the world a choice: to continue as we are, in the old, greedy, selfish, very human ways, and destroy ourselves, or to demonstrate at last the divine potential in every person by grasping the realities of life: the fact of the oneness of the soul; of the oneness, therefore, of humanity as a group of souls in incarnation. This will be a revelation for most of humanity.

Millions of people already believe in the soul, believe in the idea of the soul, but have very little notion, it seems to me, of what the soul really is. For most Christians, and not only Christians, the soul is a very wonderful, beautiful, powerful, divine entity who lives up in 'heaven' and who, when we die, we come before and know for the first time. And that is the end of it; we go on then as souls with a harp if we like. And one day at the end of the world the Christ will descend, and there will be a great rapture in 'heaven'.

It is a beautiful idea, but it is a mystical idea. The truth is even more beautiful, more wonderful: that divinity can be, is scheduled, planned to be, manifest on the physical plane. That is a greater mystery and a greater beauty than any rapture in 'heaven'. To bring the reality of the soul, that divinity, onto the physical plane and to demonstrate it as a Master, or a Krishnamurti, or a Leonardo da Vinci, is, it seems to me, a far greater mystery and beauty than the mystical idea of union in 'heaven'.

That will be a sudden revelation for humanity. We will know that we are souls. It will be presented to us in such a way that we will immediately grasp its reality and will feel this divinity in ourselves. The Christ Principle, the energy which Maitreya embodies, will flow out, as He has said, in tremendous potency. It will be as if, He says, "I embrace the whole of humanity". That will be an extraordinary experience for all of us.

Purpose and meaning

"For these precious minutes," the Master says. *"Each, singly, and solemnly alone, will know for that time the purpose and meaning of their lives."* For the first time we will grasp, during this overshadowing, hearing the words of Maitreya, the outline of the reality of our spiritual structure as spirit, reflected as souls, involved on the physical plane as the human personality. That will become clear, grasped suddenly, if not completely understood, by millions of people for the first time – a tremendous event for most people, hearing ideas which those interested in the esoteric teachings have taken as a matter of course, even if they do not actually understand and experience them as a reality.

Each one *"singly, and solemnly alone"* will know this for that little time, when Maitreya is overshadowing the world, maybe half an hour, 35 minutes at the most. For that time the world will stand still. Nothing else can be done, everyone will be listening, experiencing the ideas, looking at themselves as He speaks from heart to heart, so that their attention is focused in their reality, in their Beingness in the heart, not in their sense of themselves as Mr Smith or Mrs Johnson or whatever. Suddenly, during that time, humanity will experience itself for what we really are, souls in incarnation, divine beings.

Then, having given us the sense of our divinity, He will present the challenge to that divinity. He will talk about the needs of the world: the fact of the starving millions, "a blasphemy in men's midst", as the Master calls it. He will show that problem to be the first priority awaiting a renewed and regenerated humanity. He will show that without addressing the problem of hunger and starvation in the midst of plenty we will never take one step forward in the demonstration of the divinity of which He is giving people a sense, perhaps for the first time. As we are listening we will feel ourselves to be divine. We will know ourselves to be quite different from what we thought. We will remember our childhood feelings. The Master puts it so beautifully: *"Each, singly, and solemnly alone, will know for that time the purpose and meaning of their lives, will experience anew the grace of childhood, the purity of aspiration cleansed of self."*

The beauty of the child is that it has all the aspiration of a soul in incarnation. Not in the slightest way sullied with scepticism, with cynicism. It knows that this is what is best for the world. It says: "If there is illness in the world, it should be 'magicked' away. Would it not be wonderful if we could magic away all the ills of the world?" Every child wants, and uses the idea of magic, to get rid of the ills of the world – a totally unselfish aspiration. When the heart speaks, when the energy of the Christ, flowing through the hearts of humanity, awakens in each one of us that early, pure aspiration, the world will turn to Him.

Joy

"For these precious minutes, men will know afresh the joy of full participation in the realities of life; will feel connected one to another, like the memory of a distant past."

People will realize for the first time that, up till then, they have only played at life. They have never really touched the core of what life is really about; perhaps as children, yes, but never with that simple, direct, spontaneous experience of what is, what life actually is at this moment, in a way the child automatically, instinctively does. Everything of that full, rich, total absorption in, concentration on, the moment-to-moment experience of life as it is, is covered up by tensions, by 'busynesses', by all the worries and the problems which surround every adult human being in the world. Few can, for long, experience total enjoyment of the beauty of life, total absorption in that reality.

For that time, for that half hour or whatever it is, the whole of humanity will experience that childhood joy of being truly *alive*. And of being alive, not simply a physical aliveness, a sense of well-being, of good health, but a sense of being whole, connected to the reality of life on all its different levels. That is new, and yet people will feel: "That's it, and it is to do with everybody." They will feel connected to one another even though they do not see one another because they will know that everyone in the world is undergoing the same experience; some, of course, to a greater and some to a lesser extent. Some will be worried by everything they hear. Others will open their hearts and drink it in and experience it for the bliss which it is.

"Like the memory of a distant past." People have, at the very seat of their consciousness, the sense of past lives, past experiences, of soul experience, of life out of the body, as well as life on the physical plane. That lies at the core of the consciousness of every single being. And at that moment, they will experience a connectedness with all their previous experience as a person, and that contact they will know to be the reality for everyone. We are all parts of one great Oversoul. On the physical plane that fact gives the sense of brotherhood, of connectedness, and in the case of most people, *"like the memory of a distant past"*, something from way, way back will register and they will say: "Yes, that's the truth! That's how it

is." The truth of what Maitreya is saying will in an energetic, and also in a consciousness, and a memory sense, become one experience. The words, the meaning of the words, the information, and the actual experience of the Christ Principle will awaken all of that in everybody.

"Suddenly, men will realize that their life till now was a shallow thing, lacking, for the majority, all that makes life dear: brotherhood and justice, creativeness and love."

Few there are who know what brotherhood is, and justice is a dream dreamt by many, struggled for by many, and, so far, never achieved on a world scale. Some have achieved a relative degree of justice: trade unions have fought for justice in their industrial life; people have fought for political justice, for economic justice. For ever, it seems, most people have been struggling for justice, because it is the number one concept in the human mind. It means right relationship; that is the meaning of justice. People know instinctively at their best and highest moment that the meaning of life is to demonstrate right relationship. But how can we, when there is not justice?

Some people are strongly fired and motivated by injustice. Others suffer injustice for a long time before they react. But everyone, at the core of their being, longs for justice. I cannot imagine anyone who, just for the sake of it, would like injustice. They may go along with it, they may actually bring it about by their selfish actions, but no one puts it forward as the best possible relationship we could have. They would not be so stupid; they would know that no one would believe them. Justice is taken, like love is taken, as an expression of the nature of our divine being. And it is indivisible. There is only one justice, one love, one freedom, and that is what people long for. They long for justice, even though they may do the opposite. People long, very often, for what they themselves are the least able to demonstrate. But because of that, they long for it. They long for what they know is badly expressed in their behaviour, in their nature. It is the basis of guilt. It can also be the basis of great revolutionary endeavour.

"Many will know for the first time that they count, that they matter in the scheme of things."

Most people, everywhere, have the idea that they are not worth anything unless they are born into a rich family or into a powerful situation. Unless they are equipped with a powerful brain and a large ambition and the drive, the energy, to bring fulfilment of their desire, they think that they do not count. They feel like 'also-rans'. For centuries our unjust political and economic structures have created this illusion that most people have: that they do not count. They are just nobodies, peons, peasants, 'the workers', drones, there for the benefit of others.

If you are born into a powerful situation, if your father is rich, if he can leave you a lot of money, or a position of power, if you can start from such a situation, the tendency, unless you are a remarkably advanced individual, is to indulge yourself in that situation – to take advantage of the injustices which that creates and to strengthen them. The desire principle of the personality (I do not mean in every case of course; there have been wonderful reformers) has been used to further the advantages which the powerful already possess. That is why the world changes so slowly. There are many powerful people in the world who know the changes that the world needs, but who never seek to put them into effect. On the contrary, they often tend to strengthen the disadvantages for others which they clearly see. They tend to make their fortunes grow greater, their positions stronger. It is for them a self-defensive process. They are maintaining, or are trying to maintain, the status quo. The status quo is about to change in every aspect of life; the time has come to manifest these changes. For this very reason alone, much that Maitreya will say will be very unpleasant hearing for a great many presently powerful and privileged individuals.

Self-esteem

"An unfamiliar sense of self-esteem will replace their present hopelessness. Drugs of all kinds will cease their hold on men."

Most people take to drugs because they have a sense of hopelessness. They are suffering, as Maitreya says, from "spiritual starvation". They see no hope, no future. Nothing that they do ever seems to work. They are often so low in the social scale that there is no possibility that they could achieve what probably they are longing for: power, riches, admiration, love, affection, all the things that everyone longs for but which few people really achieve. It takes a lot of energy, a lot of what is called 'luck', and a lot of hard work to achieve the ambitions which many people on drugs have, but cannot possibly attain. They know they do not have the energy, the advantages. Unless they can get off the drugs, there is no hope whatsoever. Being on drugs, they do not have the ambition, only the *idea* of the ambition. Above all, they do not have the *will* to get out of that situation. If the will is not applied to the situation, nothing can change. But when a sense of self-esteem takes the place of the hopelessness, then everything is possible. And when the social, political, and economic changes go along with this new-found self-esteem, and establish a norm in which everyone has a place, in which everyone counts, we will have an entirely new society.

"Quietly, men's tears will flow in humble gratitude and longing for the good."

People are cynical, but inwardly they are not really cynical. Most people, the vast majority of people everywhere, long for the good. They long for the good because they know it is the only thing that is worth having. They know that what we call right relationship, right human relations, is not only the next predestined achievement of humanity, but that it is good, something to look forward to, something which is needed.

Everyone longs for love, for affection, for harmony, for the establishment of conditions in which their creativeness can manifest. For most people this is not available. For most people, creativeness is a dream, something that died in childhood, before they even had a chance to be creative. That is the reality for most of the 6.3 billion people in the world. People who have the opportunity, the education, and the background, financial or otherwise, to be creative are the relatively few; they are the lucky ones. It is not because they are superior, it is because of a coming together of various circumstances which determine whether some people will have that kind of 'luck' or whether they will be relegated to the dustbin.

It is mainly a political/economic problem. It is a spiritual crisis through which humanity is going today: we do not know who we are. We have forgotten the reality of our being. That spiritual crisis is focused through the political and economic fields, and unless we can create spiritual political and economic institutions, we will not know peace or justice, and human evolution would cease on this planet. That is the nature of the crisis: to discover who we are.

In these minutes, in that half hour, people will realize who we are. Each individual, as he or she experiences this overshadowing by Maitreya, experiences the Christ Principle, and awakens to what He is saying, and to the reality of their own spiritual nature, will say: "Yes, that's it! I want this! I want it because it is the good. This is what I have always wanted. I remember when I was a little boy, a little girl, I would dream of this for the world. And I have forgotten it. I haven't given it a thought in all these 30, 40, 50 years." People will awaken anew to their early aspiration for right relationship. People want this between themselves and others. They long for it, they know it is right. Everyone inwardly longs for that sense of justice, of goodness, of right relationship, of freedom for everyone. And *"tears will flow in humble gratitude"*.

"From that time onwards, a new spirit of sanctity will prevail upon the Earth."

From that moment, and for a time, this sense will carry forward. This day, this experience of half an hour, or however long it is, will carry on in people's hearts. They will feel refreshed as never before. They will feel: "Oh, it must be wonderful to be like this all the time. I remember, this is how I felt when I was a child."

People will feel again that freshness and vitality and uplifted spirit, blitheness, which children have, but which most adults have lost. Because they go around with their worries: "How am I going to pay the rent, the school fees, the doctor's bills?" People are worried to death. They are worried out of life. It is called commercialization. Commercialization has taken over from real life. That is why Maitreya calls it "more dangerous than an atomic bomb". It steals life from the people. It takes their life until every drop is out, like a squeezed lemon.

"Men will walk on tiptoe for a time."

Isn't that beautiful? *"Men will walk on tiptoe"*. Don't make too much noise, it might break this marvel. Keep your voices down. Don't shout. Let me keep this in my heart. People will not know what to do with themselves. They will want to keep this feeling, which, of course, will not last for ever. But it will last for some time, and this sense that they have touched divinity will remain.

Spirit of sanctity

"A new spirit of sanctity will prevail upon the Earth."

When they see Maitreya, and when you see Maitreya, you will know what the Master means. I would say, above all, the quality surrounding Maitreya is holiness, sanctity. He embodies, to my mind, everything that you can imagine about God. He is not God, of course (except in the sense that we are all God), but He is imbued with the holiness, the sanctity of God; pure love and will and wisdom surround Him as an aura. That is what radiates and will radiate out on that day. He will evoke that same sense in all the people, or most of the people, listening to Him and experiencing His energy on the Day of Declaration.

The sense that life is sacred will be renewed in people's minds and hearts. For a time, no one will want to disturb the feeling that we have seen life in a new way, that it is sacred, sanctified, and it is up to us to demonstrate that: to get rid of all the mess that prevents that sanctity from demonstrating. Maitreya will tie together the political, economic and social problems with the demonstration of the sanctity of life. People will grasp that, and will *"walk on tiptoe for a time"*. It is beautiful.

Soon, however, men will realize that it is not so easy; the problems will still be there. Just because the Christ is in the world, you cannot turn away from the problems, which are real. We are living on the physical plane, and though, for a time, people will experience divine sanctity and know that to be the true quality of life, they will also know that to demonstrate that sanctity, life on the physical plane must be changed. No longer can we watch millions of people slaughtering each other, or starving to death in the midst of plenty.

"Men will realize that the changes needed in the world are vast, manifold", very complex indeed, and very many of them, *"requiring patience and dedication, imagination and trust"*.

People will have to believe that Maitreya and the Masters know what They are talking about. They have to take on trust that these changes will really transform their life. They have to realize that the major obstacles to the continuous demonstration of that divinity, which, for half an hour, they experienced, are the old political and economic divisions in the world – with millions starving, others living no better than animals. They have to see that though they are far away, in Africa, India, or South America, not next door, these problems must be tackled. And people will wake up to the reality of life.

Rehabilitation

"Before long men everywhere will engage themselves in the work of reconstruction, the rehabilitation of the world."
The Masters will galvanize, with Their spiritual energy, all around Them. Their insight into the problems and into their solution will be clear-cut and logical. Their disciples, men and women everywhere, will be elected into positions of influence and power – by the democratic method – and they will put into effect the needed changes.

People everywhere will engage themselves in this work. *"Succour for the poor and hungry will take pride of place."* Maitreya says that the number one priority is to rid the world for ever of starvation. *"And so will end for ever a blasphemy in men's midst."* The ending of starvation, the feeding of the hungry, the rehabilitation of the poor, is the number one priority after the Day of Declaration. It has to be tackled on a major scale. A new United Nations agency will be set up to deal with this. At its head will be a Master, or at least a third-degree initiate, and it will, through its actions, reconstruct the world; the sharing of the world's produce will go forward apace.

Humanity, of course, has to accept this. Our free will will never be infringed. Governments will turn to Maitreya, and the other Masters when They have become known, and ask: "What do we do, what is your advice?" Because of the vastness of the problems, and the urgency of the need, all resources will be galvanized. The efforts of the aid agencies up until now will be as drops in the ocean compared to what will be achieved in the first months and year or two after the Day of Declaration.

"Millions will know for the first time the quiet happiness of satisfied need."

When we are hungry we buy something to eat. We go to a restaurant or we look in the refrigerator. Quiet satisfaction, we do not think twice about it. But if you are living in the Developing World, if you are one of the 1,300 million people who live in *absolute poverty*, if you are one of the 38 million who are literally starving to death, you cannot do that.

So will end what the Master calls *"this dark chapter in the history of the race"*. *"No more will the dying forms of the starving disgrace the screens of the affluent. No longer will men watch their brothers dying before their eyes."* That is a tragedy which has gone on for so many years, for as long as I can remember.

"Changes, unequalled in extent, will engage men's minds and hearts; naught but the finest of the past will prevail against the onslaught of the new."

Whatever stands in the way of the new energies, the new structures which these energies will create – to do with synthesis, sharing, justice, freedom for all, in every country without exception – whatever stands in the way of that achievement, will go down, will not prevail.

"Only the finest of the past ..." Of course, there is always good at the end of every age. The achievements of the age, the aspirations of the millions, the readiness to share, the aid agencies, organizations like the United Nations and the various international groupings which, behind the scenes, unite people with people and give a sense of internationalism and co-operation, will be maintained and will grow; they can only

flourish in the new situation. But those which stand in the way, those narrow, nationalistic structures based on competition, market forces and greed, will find it impossible to stand against the *"onslaught of the new"*, the ideas of the new time.

First to go will be the world's stock markets. They are, as Maitreya has said, about to crash. They will come down because they stand in the way of right relationship. They really bear no relation to the needs even of trade between countries. They are an anachronism, what Maitreya calls, very accurately, "gambling casinos" which have no part to play in the future time, at least in their present form.

"Daily, the transformations will be recorded for men to compare and admire."
Instead of watching all these soap operas and sitcoms, you will switch on and see what is happening in Rome, Moscow, Tel Aviv, and Seattle. What new marvel has been achieved in the world, what new record has been broken in achieving parity, justice and right relationship? This will be recorded and shown on a daily basis. People will register this and compare, and say: "We have not done that yet. We have to do that." This is the kind of competition and rivalry which will be a very positive stimulus to securing these goals. People will say: "If they can do it, we can do it." And so up will go the score cards every day: achieved ending of hunger in such-and-such and such-and-such. People in so-and-so rehabilitated, rehoused, and so on. All of this will be recorded, so everyone will be kept informed of the transformations which are taking place. *"A new world will be constructed in the blazing light of day."*

"For many, the very presence of the Christ will constitute a problem." There are many people who hate this whole idea, who do not want change. *"Their long-held beliefs will be shaken to the core,"* when the Christ appears on television and

26

forms a telepathic link with humanity and says: "I am the World Teacher, I am the one you are awaiting." Perhaps He will say something like this, I do not know. In some way He will make it known that He is the One expected by everyone, even though they do not know they are expecting Him.

Some will have a very difficult time. *"For them, a period of heartsearching will be inevitable as they seek to understand the meaning of the new dispensation; ancient beliefs die hard and hurt bitterly in the process."* If you are a fundamentalist Christian, Hindu, Buddhist, Muslim or whatever (and for those people, to be fair, their religion is serious; they hold these beliefs in a very serious, if fanatical, way), this is going to be very disturbing. Many of them believe, now, that Maitreya is the antichrist. They are really going to be shaken when they see what they think is the antichrist speaking to them with a beautiful, wonderful vision of the future. And they will not know whether to believe it or not.

They will have the same experience, they will feel His energy, they will know that this man is embodying the energy and it does not feel bad. It feels good, actually, it is like when they go to church, only better, more so. They are going to have a problem.

Then they will see all the changes in the world. Eventually, so many people will be involved in the changes, so respectable will this whole experience become, that they will find it more and more difficult to stand against it. It will be a sad time for fundamentalists because they will see the end of their beliefs. They will have to replace them with all these New Age ideas. They will have to accept that those 'New Age' types were telling the truth, talking sense, that it was not some attack, a conspiracy, which was going to be imposed on humanity by the antichrist.

"Ancient beliefs die hard" – and they have had them for hundreds of years – *"and hurt bitterly in the process. Nevertheless, millions will respond with a glad heart, happy to accept the Teacher in their midst. Few, in time, will stand against the common acknowledgment that the Christ, in the person of Maitreya, walks once more upon the Earth."*

What a realization for humanity. If you are prepared in advance, you do not experience it. We are going to miss out in a way, because we know about this. We have run through this scenario already, we have lived it. There will be plenty of revelations but we will miss out on this sudden new awakening to a reality which we take for granted – although the actual experience of it will be such as you cannot begin to imagine. When you feel His energy pouring through your heart chakra, when you hear His words in your head in your own language, you will say: "I never thought it would be like this. I never imagined it could be so powerful and so transforming."

"Those relatively few who have led the way in preparation for this time will find themselves offered another field of service: an educational endeavour vast in scope."

Do you realize what it means? The vast majority of humanity do not know anything about this, and will want to know. They will ask: "Who is Maitreya? Where does He come from? What is the historical background to all of this? And, if what He says is true and the world is going to be changed in all these ways, where do I stand? What is going to happen to my stocks and shares? What about my job?" It is going to be traumatic for most of us.

"An educational endeavour vast in scope. From all sides will come the queries." We shall become an information booth. *"A long-felt hunger for knowledge will, like a dammed-up river, overflow and burst its banks."*

People are hungry for knowledge. People who will not give much time to this information now will suddenly discover that they have an appetite for information such as they never knew. They will not be able to get enough, and they will not be able to digest what they get, so they will want more and more.

"Many will seek to know the background and history of this event. For others, the immediate future will be the chief concern."

How will this work out? What has Maitreya, or the Masters, to say about this? What do you think is going to happen? How will it be? What task can I do? What should I learn? How should I develop myself?

"Societies, worldwide, will play their part, assuring the broad dissemination of the needed teachings."

We are not the only group in the world who knows the esoteric teachings. We share this knowledge with many societies and groups, some of them far older than ours, who have long played a part in informing humanity about the reality of Hierarchy, of the evolutionary process, the human spiritual constitution, and so on.

The most important piece of knowledge that everyone needs, I believe, is the knowledge of the spiritual constitution of humanity. Everyone needs to know that they are the Monad, the Spark of God, the Divine Self, which reflects itself on the soul plane as the individualized human soul (part of one great Oversoul) which incarnates – through the Law of Rebirth in relation to the Law of Karma – over and over again until it has completed the evolutionary journey and is perfected. That is the fundamental information which, I believe, every single man and woman needs to know. When they do, that alone will give them a grasp of the true relationship between each other and between them and God. From there, the educational work can proceed. Meditation, as the means of reuniting these separated units, will become the aim of many. But people have to be educated, have to learn to do these things, to see the reality of them. That is an ongoing educational task.

Many societies will play their part, the Master says, *"assuring the broad dissemination of the teachings."* He says: *"Much remains to be given."* Maitreya will teach, probably on a daily basis, I do not know, but frequently. He has already given a body of teachings which were published in *Share International* magazine. This teaching will go on both from Maitreya and by some of the Masters. But the Master says: *"Much already remains unopened and unread in the hands of men."* There is a vast body of teachings – the Theosophical teachings, the Agni Yoga teachings, the Alice Bailey teachings – which is largely unread, even by those who know about them.

I am astonished by people's lack of interest in the information, which is available to them in, for example, the Alice Bailey teachings. People ask me questions which are easily answered if they would just turn to the right book. But people are lazy, they want me to do their reading for them. I am amazed at the lack of reading of the existing material. You have to read in order to know, and you have to digest what you read. So you have to read it with care.

How can you know anything if you do not study it? You have to learn to study. You have to do what the Master says: *"Systematic study of the teachings and earnest attempts to live the precepts of Maitreya, will give the needed balance and authority with which to teach."* How can you possibly teach others if you do not know yourself? You have to learn, in order to pass it on to other people.

Also, *"earnest attempts to live the precepts of Maitreya"*. Nothing convinces so much as the authority of experience. If you have already experienced something, you can talk about it. Even if you have difficulty putting that experience into words, the words you do say to describe your experience of a lived knowledge will communicate itself to the listener in a way that nothing else could do. No amount of simple book learning can take the place of living. Anyone can read a book. But only if you have lived the precepts, have tried to put, to the best of your endeavour, the precepts of Maitreya into effect in your life, will it have that persuasiveness, that energy of true livingness which you want the teaching to convey. The teaching will only mean something to people if it is living, and it is only living if it is part of your true experience, not simply out of a book. If it has affected and changed your life, then you can talk about it, you can make it real and living to other people in a way which otherwise is impossible.

Humble pride

"Each one, thus equipped, can avail themselves of this opportunity to serve anew. Seize it," the Master says. *"Seize it, the counsel is, with alacrity and humble pride."* That is lovely. Humble pride. That is the way forward for the groups. If you wish to serve in the new way after the Day of Declaration, you will find a world out there longing for information, for experience: longing to participate, to know what meditation is and how they can be involved, longing to know what the experience of others has been, how they entered it, and how it has changed them.

They will want to know because everyone after that day, the Day of Declaration, will realize that the world will never be the same again. A new world, a new dispensation, a new civilization, will gradually grow. What, till now, we have taken for granted will be swept away. I do not mean the first day, but fast. People will demand the new insights, the new teaching, the new revelations. They will come, of course, mainly from Maitreya and the Masters. But everyone who has any claim to discipleship has a part to play, can put their energy into spreading the teachings, as needed, as they are called for.

QUESTIONS AND ANSWERS

MAITREYA'S EMERGENCE

"On the Day of Declaration, the world will know that
I, Maitreya, Son of Man, now dwell among you. I have
come to show you the possibilities which, as sons of
God, lie before you. My heart knows your response,
teaches Me your choice, and awakens great gladness."
(Maitreya, from Message No. 137, *Messages from
Maitreya the Christ*)

Q. Is there any specific date for Maitreya's appearance?
A. Most people imagine that world events (and the coming of
a World Teacher is certainly a world event) take place according to precise dates. They imagine that all Hierarchical
decisions are designed for dates written in stone. This is assuredly not the case. The Masters predict certain happenings to
take place around a certain time, but They know that humanity has freewill and therefore has an enormous influence on
the precise timing of a given event. The Masters work in 2,000
year cycles, so for Them really precise timing is not a major
consideration. No one knows the exact date on which Maitreya
will take up His open work, but everyone can understand that
it is very soon.

'Windows of opportunity'

As far as Maitreya is concerned, there is no set date, not even
to appear on television. There are 'windows of opportunity'.
These windows are constantly changing. They are the result
of His understanding of the cosmic energies as they flow.
These are positive and negative, and they change all the time.
This is the difficulty for Maitreya. With all His insight and wis-

dom – and two levels of cosmic consciousness – and over-shadowed by two colossal Avatars (Spirit of Peace or Equilibrium and Avatar of Synthesis), with the cosmic understanding that that gives Him, He sees the window of opportunity as only a possibility. As soon as it approaches, something else can happen to change the scene again. This occurs over and over again.

He can see there will be a window of opportunity coming up on the horizon, because certain cosmic energies will be flowing and should sustain themselves for some set cycle. But is humanity ready in that window of opportunity? Are the media responsive then? What other factors we cannot even begin to imagine does He have to take into account as making up that window of opportunity? We should rid our minds of this sense of impatience. What is the date for the Day of Declaration? Maitreya, Himself, does not know. I do not mean He has no idea, but the Masters do not think in time so it is irrelevant to set a date.

What He sees is a series of windows in which all the forces which make up the statistics whereby He can judge a moment have to be taken into account – all these different things like the state of humanity, what we do for ourselves, and especially the activity of the Lords of Materiality, the forces of chaos, who are not sitting twiddling their thumbs. They are active as never before, because they know their time is over – as soon as Maitreya comes forward, and humanity sees the Masters and begins the process of reconstruction, lifting humanity above the level where they can be influenced. Through their agents: men and women in the world, some of them very well known in the media and other fields; the leaders of certain countries; certain groups of financiers who are set against this happening; various reactionary groups, political and religious, these destructive forces work to prevent the Christ's open appearance.

They know what is happening, they know that it is not good for them and they are resisting it for as long as they possibly can. There are some well known people who are resisting all they can the externalization of the Hierarchy, because for them it is the end of their power. They are men dominated by power. Their main interest is the sustaining of that power over their employees by the thousands, and the minds of people in their millions all over the world. They are power-hungry men whose only real interest in life, apart probably from making money, is to have power over the minds of others and to regulate their ideas in the way they see as right: the old, greedy, selfish, separatist way of the past. In a sense, they cannot help themselves. They are dominated by their nature and their energies, and they put up a great bulwark against this externalization process. It will not work; it is inevitable that it will not work – it is only a question of time.

Q. Why is Maitreya taking so long to manifest openly?
A. Maitreya seems to be taking a long time. From our point of view it is a long time. From the Masters' point of view, it is like the blink of an eye. What Maitreya has been waiting for, above all, is the actual collapse of the world's economic system, the breakdown of the bourses around the world. These represent the great disease of humanity – that is, speculation. Humanity is speculating all the time in order to become richer – we are focused on becoming rich. We have descended into a depth of materiality which is now dangerous for the continued existence of ourselves and the world. Maitreya calls it the blind following of market forces. He says that market forces have their role, but the blind following of market forces leads only to destruction. He calls market forces the 'forces of evil' – because they have in-built, inherent in them, division, separation, inequality – they benefit the rich and the few at the expense of the many.

Q. How long will it be before Maitreya takes up his place as world ruler? Is there some force opposing him?

A. Firstly, a correction. Maitreya will not take up a post as 'world ruler'. He does not come to rule; He comes only to teach and inspire. Humanity must learn to rule itself under the inspiration of the teachers. The exact timing of His emergence into world affairs is not written down or known precisely, even to Maitreya. It depends on the response of humanity to His teachings, to their readiness to change and to the collapse of the existing economic structures, which alone will bring us into reality. When these things are sufficiently advanced, Maitreya has said He will assuredly make His presence known. Even when He first speaks openly on television, He will not use the name Maitreya, thus giving humanity the opportunity to respond to His call for sharing, justice and peace through identity with His ideas, rather than His name or position.

The forces opposing are many and tremendously strong. They are the forces of age-long greed, selfishness and complacency. They are also the nefarious forces who for millennia have held humanity in thraldom to these same evils. However, there has never been a Teacher, an Avatar, of such tremendous power. As Maitreya says: "The end is known from the beginning." The success of His mission is assured.

Q. In Benjamin Creme's first book, **The Reappearance of the Christ and the Masters of Wisdom**, *he writes: "the Day of Declaration ... will be about 18 months from now, May 1982." Here it is 22 years later, and nothing. How can you make such irresponsible claims?*

A. The original plan of Hierarchy was that Maitreya would reveal Himself by the end of May 1982 if the world's media would go through a token, symbolic, act of looking for Him and inviting Him forward. To make this possible, I was asked to hold a press conference, reveal where Maitreya was living, and invite the media to make this symbolic act on behalf of humanity in general. I held the press conference in Los Angeles on 14 May 1982. All the main American media were present plus the BBC from London. Over 90 media representatives heard me present my information and reveal that Maitreya lived in the Asian community of London. I challenged them to send journalists to London, make the symbolic search and Maitreya would come forward to them. The media, unfortunately, did nothing, and the long, long way of emergence had to be undertaken by Maitreya so that humanity's free will was not infringed.

The interesting thing is that infinitely more people are aware of the need for change in the world along the lines of Maitreya's ideas, and more expectant to see and work for Him, than in 1982. Audiences at my lectures are very many times greater than they were then. Perhaps humanity was just not ready for Maitreya in 1982.

Q. Is it because the media have difficulty relating our information to the facts that they do nothing? Is it a lack of facts or evidence or what?
A. It is a fact that Nelson Mandela, after 27 years' incarceration, was suddenly released and became the president of the new South Africa. It is a fact, and the prediction about it was published in *Share International* [September 1988]. Maitreya visited Nelson Mandela in his cell and told him to write a letter to President de Klerk suggesting a meeting to discuss the future of South Africa. Nelson Mandela laughed and said: "I cannot even get a meeting with the governor of the prison let alone the president of the Republic." Maitreya said: "Yes, I know that. But write the letter anyway. You write the letter and I will do the rest." And He did the rest. He approached the president while he was at prayer and He put in his mind that the time had come to end apartheid in South Africa. The president

was praying, and he took it to heart. He thought it was God answering his prayer. He was a sincere Christian. He talked to God, asking what he should do and he got the answer: "The time has come to end apartheid." And we know the results.

These are facts, you see. Now, the media either believe that or they do not, but the whole thing is an extraordinary story. And they know it is. These are men whose whole lives are spent on stories.

When I held a press conference, speaking to a group of nearly a hundred journalists, on 14 May 1982 in Los Angeles, I gave the whole story and these journalists were very mixed. Some were complete fundamentalists in their own way. Some were totally against it, but many of them were open. They clapped several times about the need for sharing and justice in the world – hardheaded journalists who never clap for any-body. They clapped this story of mine, this simple story, and at the end I talked about journalists coming to London and going through the motions of looking for Maitreya, and that He would come forward to them if they did that.

The BBC had linked this press conference with a pro-gramme which was broadcast at the same time. They were there on the spot in London where I said Maitreya was living. When the American media asked the BBC what they were doing about it, the British media said: "Nothing." The Americans said: "But why not? It is a fantastic story." The BBC said: "We know it is a fantastic story but we are waiting for more tangible evidence." The "more tangible evidence" they could only get by doing what I asked them to do: come to London and go through the motions of looking for Maitreya in the Asian community.

If these journalists had been men of 'clout' who, having seen Maitreya would believe, they would speak to their col-leagues and say: "Yes, it is true. The story is true. I met him. He is extraordinary." Maitreya said that would have been enough in 1982. The media want the information put in their lap. We put the information in their lap, but that is not enough. They want to see Maitreya, and as soon as He raises His head above the parapet they will act.

There are many journalists who met Maitreya at the conference which He held in April 1990 in London. There were about 40 really important journalists present. They know it as well as I do. They will not take the responsibility of doing anything about it because their jobs are at stake. They have wives and family responsibilities. It is not easy.

Q. How do you explain the contradictions between the comments of the Master Djwhal Khul in **The Externalisation of the Hierarchy** *[by Alice A. Bailey] and your position about the Reappearance preceding the externalization?*

"The first step is the appearance of certain Ashrams, controlled by certain Masters, upon the physical plane, evoking general recognition and guaranteeing to the public the fact of the Hierarchy and the restoration of the Mysteries. Later, if these steps prove successful, other and more important reappearances will be possible, beginning with the return of the Christ."

A. I simply make known my experiences as I have been asked to do. The plans of Hierarchy are often detailed and exact but also fluid and adaptable to changing circumstances. The entry of Maitreya in July 1977 was preceded by the externalization of five Masters into New York, London, Geneva, Darjeeling and Tokyo in 1975. These Masters have not sought to "evoke general recognition", but They work closely with Their disciples in these cities and countries. There are now 14 Masters plus Maitreya in the world.

Q. When will the first appearance of Maitreya on television take place? From zero to three years from now; three to seven years from now or more than seven years?

A. What do you think? You want me to make a prophecy about it. I do not know if Maitreya knows the exact date. It is not as if They [Hierarchy] write down a date and work to that. Maitreya sees ahead the possibilities and there are thousands of possibilities. There are thousands of things He has to take into account in determining when He will appear: what will be the most propitious moment, when will there be least opposition from cosmic, and also planetary, levels.

But I will say this: in almost no time at all. You will be surprised. You will be shaken one day when you see who has appeared on television. You will ask: "Could this be the Christ?"; "Who is it? The Imam Mahdi?" But you can imagine, Maitreya is speaking at first in America, on American television – and if you have ever been on American television you will know it is not an easy thing to do because America is so conditioned to competition, to holding on to what they have, to not changing, and arranging things to suit their need for competition.

I do not know if they will immediately think He is the Christ. They might be more likely to think he is the antichrist. They have not seen or heard Maitreya. They have only seen and heard what I have said about Him. And many do not like it one bit. They do not want that kind of change. They do not even want to accept the Kyoto Protocol for climate change. They do not want any action that will stop the flow of dollars into the big US corporations. So when I speak, many think I speak for the antichrist.

But who are 'they'? 'They' tend to be, largely, the fundamentalist Christian groups – who Maitreya loves, of course. He has often appeared before them, but they do not know He is Maitreya. If they knew that they would have a shock!

America is split down the middle. There are millions who will welcome Maitreya and there are millions who will think He is the antichrist.

40

Q. (1) Is Maitreya known personally by the person who will interview Him for the first large interview in America? (2) Does this person believe that Maitreya is the World Teacher? (3) Is s/he sympathetic to your information even if s/he doesn't believe the story totally?
A. (1) No. (2) Probably not. (3) I do not know.

Q. Why will Maitreya appear in the United States instead of in other countries?
A. He will appear in other countries. He will appear first in America in such a way that He can speak to millions of people. Then in Japan. Which country do you think has the largest and most influential media network in the world? If He appears on a major network in America, He can be heard immediately by millions of people not only in the US but through the internet worldwide. Eventually, after the Day of Declaration when He is known and accepted by humanity, He will make a pilgrimage around the world.

Q. Why did Maitreya not come forward on television to prevent the war in Iraq?
A. For the Masters, human free will is sacrosanct: They never infringe it. Maitreya makes a plan and there may be thousands of different aspects to take into account in deciding what and when to do a certain thing. That plan is not set in stone; it is pliable, flexible – but human free will would never be infringed.

To initiate a war on Iraq was a decision of the US government, and for Maitreya to have appeared openly 'to prevent it' would have been an infringement of our free will, however misguided or destructive such aggression might be. It is not up to Maitreya to make or unmake our decisions. Besides, when He does come forward, He will not immediately have the influence the questioner seems to ascribe to Him.

The Law has to be obeyed. The Masters are Masters because They live by the Law – the Law of Life, of evolution.

There are things which you can do, must do, and things you must not do. We do anything. We infringe each other's free will – we murder, injure, maim – we do it with words and deeds. That is why we have problems, why we have illness, why we suffer.

Q. Was there anything that Hierarchy could do to prevent the war with Iraq?
A. No, not without infringing human free will. There is the possibility of impressing the minds of government leaders but, unfortunately, in this case, the chances of a favourable response to impression were not high.

Q. If not initially introduced by name, how will Maitreya be introduced on television in the first interviews?
A. As an ordinary man, one of us, but with ideas, advice and points of view which could help us if we listened. In the beginning it will be rather restrained and modest. On television Maitreya will not be speaking to an invited audience; He will have to be somewhat reticent so as not to frighten off his audience.

Q. How will people invite Him on television? What will His qualifications be?
A. He will have a name, but it will not be Maitreya. The point is: He does not want the ideas to be coming from a Being so high that people become devotees. He does not want devotees, He does not want followers. He says: "If you follow Me you will lose Me. If you try to put Me in your pocket you will never find me." The Christians will try to put Him in their pocket. So will Muslims, so will Hindus, and especially Buddhists. It is not a problem; if He is invited on television to speak, He can be invited on another channel to speak to more people. It is as simple as that. On the Day of Declaration He will acknowl-

edge what many people suspect but may be unsure of: that He is the World Teacher. He will be invited as Mr So-and-So to speak about his ideas. It will be restrained at first; He will not say what I am saying at first, but He will grow in intensity as people around Him respond. If He said what I would say He would drive people away from Him. He does not make a difference between fundamentalist Christians, fundamentalist Jews, fundamentalist Muslims, and so on, and non-fundamentalists. He does not make that difference. He has thousands of followers who at some level have experienced Him, and they know Him. It is hard to describe. He is totally tolerant, non exclusive.

Q. Could you clarify, once again, the 'form' Maitreya will take on television. For example, will he be a man being interviewed by the likes of Ted Koppel (well known American newscaster)?
A. Maitreya will not use His name, Maitreya, but will be interviewed as 'one of us' on major television by 'the likes of Ted Koppel', although not necessarily by Ted Koppel.

Q. If asked, would Maitreya admit to being the Christ or World Teacher?
A. At first, no. He would use some method of not answering directly, or the question would not arise. Eventually, of course, He will acknowledge His identity to more and more people. Remember that He has already met or appeared to many leaders in all branches of human affairs. They will be encouraged to come forward and make known their support. This will inevitably stimulate and embolden the masses to lend their voices to the demands for sharing and justice and so prepare the way for the Day of Declaration.

Q. Are there many diplomats, leading figures, politicians and journalists who will be encouraged to come forward after the first interview to confirm their experiences of and conviction about the identity of the Lord Maitreya?

A. I believe so, yes. Of course, it could take several interviews and some positive media reaction to inspire people of that level to come forward. There has been a terrible lack of courage so far.

Q. I read a message from Maitreya on your website in which Maitreya says He is coming so soon that it "will surprise indeed". (1) Does this mean that all conditions for His public work have been met? (2) Is Maitreya referring to a major interview when He says this?

A. (1) Nearly. (2) Not necessarily major.

Q. When Maitreya begins to make His media appearances, even though He won't be stating Who He is at first, would it be advised for co-workers who recognize Maitreya not to point Him out to people outside of the network (including family and friends) because it would interfere with the free will of an individual to recognize Maitreya for themselves?

A. Yes. I have several times made it clear to co-workers that this should be the procedure. It is very important, especially in relation to media, that their and others' free will is not infringed and that they respond to Maitreya for what He is saying as a man among men rather than as the Christ or World Teacher.

Q. If we think that we have recognized Maitreya when He is talking to media, but He is still undeclared as Maitreya, how should we act in relation to the media?

A. We should do nothing in relation to the media other than make known that Maitreya and His Group are in the world. It is not our task to point Him out to the media. They, like all humanity, have to make the recognition for themselves. If people believe, rightly or wrongly, that Maitreya is the Christ, the Imam Mahdi, Maitreya Buddha, the Messiah or Kalki Avatar, and accept His advice because of that, it does not mean that they are in themselves ready to make the changes which must ensue to preserve the world and humanity with it. We have to recognize Maitreya, not because we think He is Maitreya, or the Christ or the Messiah, or whoever, but because we agree with what He is saying, that we want for the world what He says is necessary for the world: justice and sharing and freedom for all people, rather than because we think He is the World Teacher or some great spiritual being.

Q. Will Maitreya look physically like Himself – that is, as He really is – when His first interview takes place, or will He be in a different 'guise' – as He usually is when He appears to people?
A. When He appears to people He is usually using a 'familiar', a created person through which some part of His consciousness manifests. But when He appears openly to the world, although not using the name Maitreya, He will appear as in fact He is, in the self-created body in which He manifests now in the world.

Q. (1) Will Maitreya look as he did in Nairobi when he makes his first television appearance? (2) What about on the Day of Declaration?
A. (1) No. (2) No.

Q. When we see Maitreya on television, your Master has said we will experience His ray or energy. Will that be like a preview of the Day of Declaration with a blessing taking place?
A. It will be a spiritual experience, but always at the level of the person. People can only take what they can take; they can only be who they are. Some people will immediately sense and

recognize Maitreya as the spiritual giant that He is. Others will respond more to what He says; it will satisfy their sense of justice and purpose. But that spiritual outflow will always take place. I doubt that it would be as strong as on the Day of Declaration.

Q. Maitreya is quoted as having said that "when this principle (sharing) is accepted, I will declare myself". That's very different from your own predictions about the television interview and the pending market crash, etc. So who's right, you or Maitreya?

A. Of course, Maitreya is right – and so am I. His declaration of Who and What He is will not take place until humanity has accepted the principle of sharing. This will lead to His appearance before the whole world on Declaration Day. The television interviews and market crash will precede that day.

*Q. (1) Is Maitreya aware, at all times, of everyone's thoughts? (2) Does He become aware when we're thinking of Him? For example, when we pick up our copies of **Share International** and read about Him, is a fragment of His attention drawn to that? (3) Could He pick up any musical instrument and play the most complicated piece? (4) Could He paint a masterpiece? Or (5) write a greater play than Shakespeare? (6) Could He sing like Elvis?*

A. (1) Yes. (2) Yes. (3) Yes. (4) Yes. (5) Yes. (6) No!

Q. How far does Maitreya's aura radiate from where He resides in London?

A. It enfolds the entire world.

Q. (1) How receptive, from the Hierarchy's point of view, is humanity at present [2002] to Maitreya's ideas? (2) Does increased fear and tension close people psychologically to His priorities?

A. (1) Twenty-five per cent are very receptive; 40 per cent are fairly receptive; 35 per cent are not receptive. (2) No, the opposite. Fear drives people to act hysterically – as in the US today – or to look for answers to the problems.

Q. (1) Does Maitreya continue to meet politicians and journalists? (2) Do the visitors ask Him questions? (3) Do they know who He is? (4) Do they connect Him to your work and information?
A. (1) Politicians, yes. Journalists, no. (2) Yes. (3) On the whole, no. (4) A few do.

Q. I am confused about Maitreya's emergence. I can understand that karmic laws are under consideration here as well as not infringing free will. It just worries me sometimes that only the agents of the 'light' forces take heed of these things. We have many crazy people ready to blow themselves up (with many others) in the supposed name of God. They seem to have no problem (or awareness) of karma, free will etc. If they pull off some major terrorist acts (nuclear, chemical or biological), it doesn't seem like the planet, or human race, will be around for the Emergence. How is that karmically correct?
A. Of course, that is precisely why this time is one of such major tension and crisis. Nevertheless, Maitreya and the Masters must obey the karmic law – even if we do not. We have to trust that Maitreya knows exactly when – and when not – to intervene, and still remain within the karmic law.

Q. Don't you think that the most important thing is not whether Maitreya will appear or not, but for us to act from the heart, perfecting our love and to express what our love says? Is not this the only way to Self-realization?
A. With respect, that sounds very nice but is it the reality? Is this approach the norm throughout the world? If yes, then why

do we have these many serious problems: poverty and starvation in the midst of plenty; wars and threats of wars; environmental breakdown; crime and drug abuse on a major scale; worldwide terrorism growing more sophisticated – the list is endless? It is obvious that the world, in general, does not act from the heart or express perfect love. Perhaps the questioner is an exception. Perhaps he or she does indeed practise the way of the heart and love in action. Perhaps is even now a Master, without the need for Maitreya and His teachings. For the rest of us, however, the help and advice of Maitreya and His group is essential if we are to survive. He is our life-line to the future.

Q. When Maitreya overshadows us on the Day of Declaration, will everyone have a physical sensation?
A. He has said that when His energy, that is, the Christ Principle, flows out, it will be as if He embraces the whole world. People will feel it – even physically. As the energy of the Christ Principle flows through the four levels of the etheric body to the lowest plane – which is just above physical gas – it will be felt on the physical body as a resounding vibration. If you are at all aware of the etheric body, you will experience this as a very powerful physical sensation. Otherwise, you will probably feel it as a pressure on the top of the head during the overshadowing. Then you will hear His words inwardly in your own language.

*Q. It says in the **Bible** that Christ will return in a "blaze of Glory". Where was Maitreya's blaze of glory that we could all see and recognize?*
A. This "blaze of Glory" is, of course, a symbolic term for His spiritual stature recognized by all. This will take place on the Day of Declaration when He overshadows all humanity.

Q. How will we know to turn the television on for the Day of Declaration?

A. You will be informed beforehand by the media. In all the different countries the media will say that they have invited Maitreya to speak to the whole world. You know the Man, Whom you have been seeing, and He will speak to the whole world simultaneously. They will link up all the networks by satellite, which are really in place for this event – not so that we can watch the World Cup, however exciting. It is so that for the first time in human history the World Teacher can come and speak directly to all humanity.

Q. What is going to happen if people don't have television?

A. They will hear it in their head – it is a telepathic rapport. You don't have to be watching television, but then you won't see His face. You may be under the car, mending the car, but you will hear His words; put that spanner down and listen!

Q. On the Day of Declaration will the Teacher's (Maitreya's) face appear to TV viewers differently (according to various races or cultures) or as the same man worldwide?

A. He will appear as the same man to all.

Q. Can children experience the Blessing on the Day of Declaration?

A. On the Day of Declaration all people above the age of 14 will hear Maitreya's words in their minds in their own language. It is not a question that younger children cannot experience His Blessing – on the contrary. But it is more a question of whether their minds can take in and relate to His message.

Until the age of 14 there is little or no mental focus in the average child, so under that age the child would not understand what he or she was hearing. But at every age, each one will understand (or not) according to their development. Maitreya knows exactly the point in evolution of any child and the state of its charkas, what it can absorb, what would be safe. Everyone's state of health, age and so on will be taken into consideration. This is the miracle of the omnipresent overshadowing.

Q. What criteria will be used to determine who will be healed or cured on Declaration Day?
A. Karma and faith. Those whose karma permits, and whose faith opens them to the energy of the Christ Principle as it flows from Maitreya, will be healed.

Q. How is it possible for Maitreya to connect with us telepathically (on the Day of Declaration) when most of us are restless and have 'broken' mental microphones? Is not this chronic condition only cured by regular and deep meditation?
A. Yes, I agree that most of us do not have the inner mental focus or magnetic aura that makes conscious telepathy possible, but the Day of Declaration must be seen as a unique event and situation for Maitreya. For Him, there is no separation. He is omniscient and omnipresent. He will overshadow the minds of humanity in such a way as to make us – temporarily – open to His message.

Q. After the Day of Declaration will everybody be aware of the fact of Maitreya's presence and that of His group, the Masters of Wisdom?
A. I cannot speak for everybody, but the vast majority of humanity will have heard His words telepathically on the Day of Declaration, and it seems obvious that the time and resources

of media from then on will be devoted to making known the advice and priorities of Maitreya. One must remember that there will be no recording of the telepathic message that Maitreya will give and no doubt there will be misremembering and misquoting of His meaning. But Maitreya will be available for clarifying in the normal way, in further interviews, the exact meaning of His words.

Q. When Maitreya has emerged openly, will He and other Masters continue to appear to people, as reported in the 'letters to the editor' in **Share International** *magazine?*
A. As necessary, yes.

Q. After Maitreya officially announces Himself to the world on Declaration Day, how long will it be before He introduces the Masters to the world?
A. Maitreya will probably introduce the idea of the Masters as His disciples during the overshadowing on the Day of Declaration. The introduction of at least some of the Masters will take place soon afterwards.

Q. Will the Master Jesus also make Himself known to the world?
A. On the Day of Declaration Maitreya will introduce, not the Masters Themselves, but the fact of Their presence. Later, the Masters will come forward one by one and make Themselves known. The Master Jesus will be one of the first to come forward.

Q. Do you think that most Christians will recognize and accept the Master Jesus, thus dispelling their fear of Maitreya as the antichrist?
A. The short answer to this question is yes, I do. Jesus is probably the best known of all the Masters and millions will

probably follow Him in the first place, perhaps indefinitely. That is fine because the aims of Maitreya and the Master Jesus are the same.

Q. Will Christians not continue to follow and worship the Master Jesus rather than Maitreya?
A. Many Christians may, after the Day of Declaration, follow the Master Jesus because they know His name. Maybe they will see the Master Jesus as the Christ and Maitreya as His lieutenant. It does not really matter. And I doubt if Maitreya would be upset!

Q. When Maitreya presents Himself to the world, how do you think people will react to Him?
A. Well, it depends who they are. It depends on their religious background. It depends, I think, whether they are Piscean or Aquarian in their thinking. The world is divided into two: those who compete and those who co-operate. He is for co-operation, but those who cannot live without competing, those of Piscean consciousness, will tend to reject the idea of sharing and justice in the world as a condition for peace. It does not mean that they want war, but they certainly do not want peace if it means giving up anything. They do not see that you cannot for ever have a just society if in some parts of the world there is the very opposite. The world is one, and the sooner all peoples realize that the sooner we will have a decent world to live in.

It depends who you are. If you are starving, if you are hungry – He is talking about feeding the starving, sharing the world's resources – are you going to follow Him or not? Of course you are. It may be that the dispossessed of the world, who are two-thirds of the world's population, will be the first to rally round Him. It will build up to a great world public opinion. That galvanized, educated, energized, properly-led public opinion is a force against which no nation can stand. It will not take long before the world is truly one, until we start creating the institutions which will outline the form of the new society.

Q. How will leaders respond to Maitreya's speech on Declaration Day?
A. It depends who they are. Who will respond to Maitreya? More important than the world leaders is the world population, men and women of goodwill, in every country without exception. Leaders do what they have to do to keep the people quiet. If people everywhere got up and demanded justice, peace and sharing, the leaders would have to respond; and in France, Britain, Germany, Japan, the USA, the leaders would have to respond or shoot them – one or the other.

There are people in high positions, in the diplomatic services, in governments, in industry, in the financial world, in religious groups, who know Maitreya is in the world. They have seen Him, they have attended a conference (in 1990 in London) where He appeared (and disappeared), and spoke to them. They know Who He is, and they are simply waiting to see His head 'above the horizon', and then they will speak out. People will follow them. The present leaders do not have to lead the way – their time is interim; they are mainly a group of people of the past and they will be relegated to the past.

How Do Maitreya and
the Masters Work?

"When the Day of Declaration dawns, you will know
that that Brother has taught you more than once, has
shown you the way to God and released the Teachings
of God's Truth. My friends, the time has come to en-
large that Truth, to show you that to know God is a
creative act, to know God is to enter into Deity Itself.
Only thus can we know the truth of our existence. In
this coming time, that knowledge will be yours."
(Maitreya, from Message No. 112)

*Q. How hands-on will Maitreya work in relation to humanity
when He is openly accepted? How much will He direct things
or will He only respond with advice?*
A. Maitreya is here to advise, guide and teach. He is not here
to direct our actions and will not do so. He is a teacher. The
Masters, His immediate disciples, will be available with Their
higher knowledge and experience for help and advice, as also
will Maitreya. But we have to want what we have to do.
Maitreya will outline the broad general direction of our thinking. That is: a sense of the oneness of humanity; the absolute
necessity for the sharing of the world's resources; and the ending of war and terrorism as a way of solving international
problems. When we show that we understand this, as much
help and advice as we can use will be provided. But we have
to want the changes for ourselves; willingly, gladly make these
changes. The Masters do not come to tell us what to do.
Maitreya has said: "I am the Architect, only, of the Plan. You,
My friends and brothers, are the willing builders of the
Shining Temple of Truth." The temple of truth being the new
civilization.

Q. Will Maitreya focus on practical matters – family, neigh-bourhood, relationships and so on?
A. Yes. He is a practical man involved in our practical problems. These are His priorities. The Masters are not mystics; we are the mystics. We mysticize everything. The Masters are Knowers of Wisdom. Knowledge plus love is wisdom. This is the 'wisdom living', the practical wisdom of living harmlessly in right relationship – that is what They are concerned with. You will find Maitreya to be very simple. He is a spiritual giant but He does not go around with His eyes turned up to heaven! He is involved in Life and the relationship of love. [For further reading on Maitreya's priorities, we refer you to 'Maitreya's Priorities' *in Maitreya's Mission, Volume Three,* Chapter 1.]

Q. What does Maitreya think is the most urgent problem in the world at present?
A. The most important action with which Maitreya is concerned is the saving of millions of people who currently die from starvation in a world of plenty. He says that nothing so moves Him to grief as this shame: "The crime of separation must be driven from this world. I affirm that as My Purpose." So the first aim of Maitreya is to show humanity that we are one and the same: wherever we live, whatever our colour, background or religious belief, the needs of all are the same.

Equally important and just as urgent is the saving of our planet from the destruction on which it is set from our misuse of the resources of the planet. Governments today are more and more becoming aware, after many years of information from scientists, that global warming is a reality. Global warming is now understood to a degree, but man's responsibility for it has not yet dawned on all the national authorities. This is one of the most important realizations that we have to make – that man is responsible for at least 80 per cent of the warming up of the planet, and if this continues it will drastically affect our daily lives. Maitreya and the Masters alone have the exact knowledge of how to proceed, but we already know the first steps to take (the need to restrict carbon emissions and so on). But the urgency of action is probably not fully realized by governments. Maitreya will emphasize how really urgent this action is. The destruction of trees on the planet – for example, an area the size of Belgium of primal forest is destroyed every year in Central and South America – has a profound effect on essential oxygen in the world.

The necessity for sharing the resources of the planet is the number one action which Maitreya will emphasize. This will create the trust which will open the way to the solution of all further problems, national and international.

Q. Just as you have said there is a step-by-step plan to save millions from starvation – first, emergency aid and then a new system of distribution through the UN – what should be the steps we take to start the process of restoring our planet? Would there be an equivalent emergency action plan first, and if so what should we do?

A. The immediate priorities are dealing with pollution and global warming. The worst, most dangerous pollution comes from our nuclear power stations and the nuclear industry in general. This must be ended as soon as possible.

Pollution, especially nuclear radiation, according to the Masters, is already the number one killer in the world. It so diminishes the activity of the immune system that people succumb to many diseases such as pneumonia, influenza, AIDS, HIV and so on. The very air we breathe, the water, the soil, is totally polluted, and we are destroying the very planet which we need for our continued existence and that of our children. One of the major things which will happen after the Day of Declaration is the turning of the attention of humanity really strongly to the cleaning up of the environment and making this

Earth viable again. Every human being, of whatever age, will be involved in this process. As soon as the needs of the starving millions are met, as soon as the process of sharing is under way, then the attention of all must turn to the support of our eco-systems, otherwise there will be no planet.

Maitreya Himself has said that the saving of the environment must become the first priority of all people, young and old. The effects of global warming on the ice caps, for example, are now evident to all. A huge programme of reforestation awaits our attention; this, of course, will take time to achieve, but a start could be made now.

Q. Given that global warming will not stop immediately, even if the 200-year supply of oil-bearing sands in Canada (figure from BBC News) and even larger supplies of coal are never burned, should we anticipate a meltdown of polar ice over the next several centuries that will make many coastal areas uninhabitable?
A. Steps will be taken to lessen that risk.

Q. Can you explain why, if global warming is a major problem, Maitreya has "brought the Earth a little closer to the Sun"? Doesn't that exacerbate the warming and, if so, can we assume that whatever climate changes do occur will not in the end prove more deleterious than if Maitreya had not performed this rather bizarre-seeming action?
A. Twenty per cent of global warming is caused by the Earth having been brought a little nearer to the sun. Eighty per cent is caused by our misuse of resources and gas emissions. Why would Maitreya do this? One has to assume that it is under Law and for the benefit of humanity. It will render large areas of northern Europe, Asia, Canada and Russia, now largely ice-bound for most months of the year, extraordinarily fertile for growing food. It also reinforces the need for action on our part to limit global warming.

*Q. In the June 2003 issue of **Share International**, in the section on Maitreya's teachings, it says: "Enjoy the warm weather, the early spring and the blossoming life around you. It has nothing to do with holes in the ozone layer or the 'greenhouse effect'. What has happened is that the pace of the Earth's rotation has slowed down and the Earth has moved closer to the sun. This is so that there can be more vegetation to feed the world." If the 'greenhouse effect' and global warming in particular are seen to be serious global problems, why does this quotation from Maitreya's teachings imply that global warming is a positive development?*

A. It is a question of degree. The slowing of the Earth's rotation is controlled and under law – the effects are predictable and within limits. The 'greenhouse effect' and global warming, the result of pollution, are, on the contrary, out of control (except by cessation of pollution) and pose environmental threats that are, to some extent, unpredictable and irreversible. [Maitreya's teachings published in *Share International* magazine are compiled in the book *Maitreya's Teachings: The Laws of Life.*]

Q. I was first introduced to the story of Maitreya in the early 1980s by a newspaper advertisement headed 'There will be no World War Three'. I have never doubted Maitreya's presence and eventual emergence, and have joined the anti-war protests, but I am now wondering if that newspaper statement was somewhat over-optimistic?

A. It is true that many people still fear a third world war, and the recent invasion of Iraq, unilaterally and pre-emptively, by America and Britain, has heightened world tension immeasurably. Longer-term ambitions by the US, as voiced openly by their most 'hawkish' leaders, do not help to build harmonious and co-operative relations. However, despite these real problems, Hierarchy have no doubt of eventually inspiring justice and therefore peace.

Maitreya, you may be certain, has not come into the world to watch its destruction. Peace, today, is not an option but an absolute necessity for humanity to survive. That being so, Maitreya, you may be sure, will use all His various means to ensure that His plan succeeds.

Q. You have said that one of Maitreya's priorities would be to find solutions to the conflict in the Middle East, and that it will not be solved until He has actually come forward. Is that because the different people involved in the Middle East (Muslims, Jews, Christians), will respond to Him as their World Teacher, and will recognize that He has come for all of them, and that their separatism will start to change from that response?

A. The Palestinian/Israeli problem, which is central to the problems of the Middle East, I believe will only be solved through the action of Maitreya. But even Maitreya cannot impose a solution; He can only advise. But His acceptance by countless millions in the world as a spiritual teacher and guide will make it easier for the most fanatical Israeli Jew or Palestinian Muslim to accept the necessity of living together side by side. This can only take place when justice is given to the Palestinians. When justice is done, and seen to be done, fully and completely, then the solution will become acceptable by the Muslims, and, even if grudgingly, by the Israelis. They have eventually to learn to live side by side, and they can only do so in a state of justice. Otherwise there would inevitably be perpetual war between the two.

Unless the Middle East problems are solved there will never be peace in the world, and we know if there is no peace then the future for humanity would be very bleak indeed. Muslims await the Imam Mahdi, and the Jews await the Messiah, and many will be ready to recognize Maitreya as such. This will, I am sure, soften their stance in relation to each other.

But the important thing is that justice must be given to the Palestinians. The West Bank was gifted by the late King Hussein of Jordan as a homeland for the Palestinians, and that means the whole of the West Bank, not the fraction which has been offered to the Palestinians so far. It requires the return of the 4.7 million refugees, mainly in Lebanon, to their home-land, and the status of Jerusalem – which is of major importance to the Muslims, the Jews and the Christians – to be changed into an open, central city for all three groups. I be-lieve it will take Maitreya to bring this reconciliation about, but so it will be.

Q. Is there any time-scale for that?
A. Well, *we* make the timescale. It is a question of the will of the people of the area: they make the timescale. If they are will-ing to make the changes, accept the resolution of the conflict and make a just peace possible, it can be very quick. It depends on the resistance of the fanatical groups on both sides. But when the whole world is being changed you will find that these small areas, however important they may be, will find it more and more difficult to resist the changes which will bring about peaceful solutions.

Essentially, everybody wants a world at peace. Only mad warmongers want war, which is good for business and makes fat profits for certain groups. But when humanity as a whole sees the absolute necessity for peace, then the end of war itself can be achieved. This is Maitreya's task, to teach humanity these facts. It's a question of putting over what people know: I know, you know, everybody knows the need for peace, but still we have wars. It's because people think that by the use of war, of some measure, they can restore the balance their way. But when the world as a whole is going in a certain direction, then you will find that small factions will follow suit.

Q. Will the Masters bring together the various religions and, if so, how?

A. Maitreya does not come as a religious teacher but as a spiritual one. All aspects of life are fundamentally spiritual; everything that benefits us, that takes us to a higher level, is, in fact, spiritual. The aim of Hierarchy is not the unification of all the religions. These will continue, although cleansed and purified by the presence of the Masters and better human understanding. There will gradually emerge, not exactly a new religion, but a new approach to Divinity through invocation rather than through worship, involving, not belief, but awareness of, and experience of, the Divine.

*Q. In your book **The Great Approach** you are asked whether the Master Who was the Prophet Mohammed is now responsible for the Islamic faith. You answered "No". But I recall you said that Mohammed would do the same for Islam (ie shake loose the man-made dogmas, etc) as Jesus would do for Christianity.*

A. The Prophet Mohammed has responsibility for Islam but is not one of those Masters Who will externalize Themselves in this coming time. The work of purification of Islam (in line with the purification of Christianity performed by the Master Jesus) will therefore be carried out by an initiate appointed by the Master Who was Mohammed.

Q. If your Master or the Christ could today address directly the United Nations Security Council and the world's leaders, what would They advise in order to cement a real and permanent rapprochement in the Middle East, and with the Muslim world in general?

A. The creation of justice and freedom through the sharing of essential resources throughout the world. Sharing is inevitable, and the sooner understood and implemented, the sooner peace and security for all will be achieved. This is true for the Middle East and the world in general.

Q. Is Maitreya putting out thoughtforms for us to respond to?
A. The Hierarchy are putting out thoughtforms all the time – the mindbelt of the world is saturated with thoughtforms, many of no value at all, created by humanity. The bulk of humanity cannot tune in at a high enough level to the thoughtforms of the Masters. But some are major ideas to which the sensitive minds of the race tune in. For instance, suddenly, all over the world, a group of scientists have the same idea, which was placed there by a Master, or even by Maitreya. The Masters see the need for a certain step forward to be taken, a certain technology, for example, to be discovered. They are the inspirers, the 'muses', of the world. Behind all the great teachers, scientists, painters and artists of all kinds have stood the Hierarchy, down through the centuries.

Rembrandt is Rembrandt because he was a third-degree initiate, inspired by his Master; likewise Titian and Mozart. Leonardo was 4.4 degrees initiate, practically a Master. All the culture of the world has been created by the initiates of the world, sent to stimulate humanity in the gradual expansion of consciousness which is evolution.

Q. Communicating with the Masters: is it something that anyone can learn to do?
A. Telepathy is a natural attribute of humanity. Everybody is telepathic, but it is largely untrained. In people who are very close, husband and wife, lovers, or mother and children, in these cases telepathy just happens. It is not something on which they rely or even think about. Telepathy as used by the Masters and those disciples who can respond is a deliberate, conscious handling of a mental faculty which we all have in potential but which is for the most part not developed. It can

be enhanced by Masters, but the Masters do not do it just for fun, or to give Themselves something to do. They only do it for a reason – because They are training somebody who has a specific job to do, to be able to communicate quickly and easily with them without going through the motions of appearing before them, which takes much more energy than a flash of thought. Thought is everywhere. The planes of mind are open to everybody. All thoughts travel on the mind planes. When thought is directed and controlled, as between a Master and a pupil, one has instant communication. Sometimes, the Masters appear to those disciples who have not yet developed the possibility of telepathic contact. When, through the natural processes of evolution, the aura of the disciple becomes magnetic, telepathy is established as a result. It is not something we learn to do. With practice it becomes more 'fluent' and usable. However, the Masters do not work on the astral planes. Therefore it is not possible to be contacted by a Master in any conscious manner until one has reached mental, rather than astral, polarization. Mental polarization begins around halfway between the first and second initiations.

Q. When a person is receiving messages from a Master, has the Master selected them for that purpose?
A. Yes. They do not do anything just by chance. Everything the Masters do has a reason behind it. They have command of tremendous energies, but they are 'miserly' with the energy. They do not waste an ounce of energy – Their energy and energy generally.

Q. Do the telepathic abilities depend on the pupil?
A. Of course, yes. If the Masters want to make contact with a disciple who can be telepathically reached they will use telepathy. If there is no reason to use it, They don't use it. The Masters, of course, have total mental control and use telepathy exclusively among Themselves.

*Q. In the **Bible's** 'Book of Revelation' there are signs to Christians listed that will show the return of Jesus Christ – nation will rise against nation, famines, earthquakes, distresses upon the world that have never been seen before. Yet, we are not to be afraid because these things must occur; and we should be glad because it means our deliverance is near. Why are none of these or other scriptural verses ever quoted by Maitreya? Yes, you teach of love for our fellow man, but what about the signs of the end of the world as predicted in the Bible?*

A. Yes, I agree, there are many scriptural references in the Christian Bible to these 'end times' in which we live, and I often quote them in discussion. But they need careful and accurate interpretation which, naturally, I give them. They are often symbolic and not meant to be taken literally. For example, and most particularly, they do not refer to the end of the world but to the end of the age – the Piscean Age – which is the astronomical reality we are currently experiencing. It is this fact which brings in to open public life not only the Master Jesus but the Christ, Maitreya, Who manifested Himself through His disciple Jesus for three years, as recounted in the Christian scriptures.

Q. Some time before his death in 1982, Swami Muktananda told a group of devotees that the day would come when America would lay waste the nations of the Middle East, but that following this a great Teacher would appear in the world, and that flowers would spring up in his footsteps in the devastation. (1) Is this what we are seeing in the Middle East now, through America's direct actions in invading Iraq, through their foreign policy and, by proxy, through their support of Israel? (2) Is the timing of Maitreya's full emergence related to current Middle East events? (3) Is this forecast by Swami Muktananda to be taken as accurate?

A. (1) Yes. (2) No. (3) Yes, more or less.

Q. Are the poor an important part of what we call 'the body of the Christ'? Could you speak more about the reality of this symbol please?

A. Since the poor are for Maitreya, probably the most important part of the 'body of the Christ', then the answer is yes.

The 'body of the Christ' means those in whom the Christ Principle is awakened. The work of Maitreya is to gather these awakened souls into groups which He will initiate into the first and second initiations in the evolutionary cycle.* This is an ongoing process. He does it now. He will speed up the process. He will travel from country to country, gathering together the groups who are ready for the first and the fewer who are ready for the second initiation. That is the 'body of the Christ'.

It includes people who are poor, people who are rich, people who are middle-class, middle-poor, middle-rich, and it means anybody in whom the divine light of the Christ, the soul of humanity, is lit. He works with that, fostering it, intensifying it, leading those to the gate of initiation. These first two initiations prepare a man or woman for the third initiation, which is taken before Sanat Kumara, the Lord of the World.

This is something, of course, which very much concerns Him, the Christ, because anyone who comes before Sanat Kumara at the third initiation had to come before the Christ at the first two initiations beforehand. It is in this sense that the Christ is 'the way' and 'the life' in Christian terminology.

The last few lives (it can be 20 or 30, which is few compared with what has gone before) of the evolutionary cycle are covered by five great expansions of consciousness. That is what initiation is. It is an expansion of consciousness, and they start at the first initiation and culminate at the fifth, the Resurrection initiation, which makes you a Master. All of the Masters have gone through these five initiatory experiences, and everyone on this planet will eventually go through the same process.

The 'body of the Christ' is Christian symbology, and it really means those in whom the Christ has found and expressed Himself – the people in whom the Christ Principle is awakened. There are groups I know, individuals and groups, who think the Christ cannot live in the world because there are not enough of 'them', that is, those in whom the Christ Principle is awakened. By 'them' they mean that they see themselves as more special than the average person. They are those who have, to my mind, a sentimental (but to them a real) idea that the Christ is a reality to them. I do not mean necessarily in a religious sense, although that might also be so, but that the Christ is awakened in them, and maybe it is. But that is so for millions of people. It is not that little group who believe that the Christ cannot be in the world because there are so few of 'them'.

The Christ is awakened, for example, in the 850,000 people in incarnation who have already taken the first initiation. That is a lot of people, so how can they be just so few, just those people in certain groups who consider themselves so enlightened and so special that the Christ cannot be in the world yet because there are not enough of 'them'.

It is a nonsense, a big glamour. There are some 850,000 people in incarnation in whom the Christ is born, who have taken the first initiation, and about 240,000 who have taken the second initiation. So the Christ is born in many. There are between 3,000 and 4,000 people in the world who have taken the third initiation.

The 'body of the Christ' are those in whom the Christ Principle is awakened. By the end of this Age that will be the vast majority of humanity who will have taken the first initiation, some the second, some fewer the third, the fourth, and fewer still the fifth.

That is the 'body of the Christ'. That is not the poor, exclusively, as was suggested in the question. There is no doubt that the poor, living in anguish for lack of the everyday necessities, for whom Maitreya has a special concern and a special warmth and feels a special responsibility, are especially dear to Him because their need attracts His love and He is the Lord of Love.

*[For more information regarding the initiations, refer to *Maitreya's Mission, Volumes One, Two* and *Three* by Benjamin Creme.]

Q. I have followed Share International for more than 10 years now. I have made donations, attended the meditations, read some of the books, read the website regularly, and seen Benjamin Creme in person in Los Angeles and London. In fact, I planned a London vacation with my family so I could attend a lecture. I am sensitive enough to feel the spiritual power around Mr Creme; this has kept me listening. However, while I find the spiritual guidance enlightening, I find the politics often misguided.

In particular I read the 'Questions and Answers' section of your magazine carefully every month and have become more and more dismayed at the political orientation of Mr Creme and Share International. It has kept me from deeper participation in the organization. Because there are so many outrageous and irresponsible assertions made that have no backing in any other source, I have begun to doubt the rest of the program.

I am not asking you to hide your orientation. It is good that you expose it so openly. However, it does limit your credibility with me and perhaps others. Best wishes in any case.

A. I am sure the writer is not alone in his dissatisfaction with the political/economic element in *Share International*. I can understand his dismay at what he sees as a greater and greater encroachment on the 'spiritual' element of the magazine by the purely 'political'. When many of the political statements are deeply critical of the present US administration and its massive contribution to the present chaos, fear and stress in the world, and the reader is American and sees US actions differently, it must be painful, vexing and embarrassing. So, too, it is for many here in Britain when we see our government lying and spinning in support of US action.

It should be remembered that our approach is never party-political, and that the questions come from readers who no doubt are seeking truthful answers which they are not getting elsewhere. Certainly, they do not all find the answers to be "outrageous and irresponsible assertions" but ones which do indeed have the backing of Hierarchy. The avowed intention of *Share International* is to bring together the two major directions of New Age thinking – the political and the spiritual – to show the synthesis underlying the political, social, economic and spiritual changes now occurring globally.

For *Share International*, everything that makes life better for humanity is spiritual, whether on the physical, the mental or the 'spiritual' plane. Why does Maitreya walk with the millions of protesters who call for political action to end war and injustice? The spiritual crisis through which we are all painfully moving is focused today in the political and economic fields. Only in these areas can it be solved and open the way for the establishment of right human relations.

Q. Spiritual teachers of the past that we know of were not associated with politics but focused on spiritual development. I am puzzled by your focus on politics. Please explain.
A. Why am I interested in politics? Because I am interested in love, in justice and freedom for everyone. Politics, economics, that is reality. That is spiritual. Where do you stop being spiritual?

When do you stop being spiritual? How do you measure the degree of spirituality in a person? Everything in life is spiritual – we live in a spiritual universe. It could not be otherwise. The trouble is, we do not make it spiritual. We have the most corrupt politics that have ever been devised, the most corrupt economic structures ever created by man. They are not spiritual but they should be, and must be, spiritual.

What I am talking about is spiritual politics, spiritual economics, and you will find that the Christ Himself, the Lord Maitreya Himself, the World Teacher, will concentrate in the beginning on politics and on economics. What I am saying comes from Him. These are His thoughts, His ideas. Politics, economics, should be the most spiritual things. Politics is about how people live together, and economics is about how we distribute the world's resources. If you are not spiritual, you do it badly, like today. Who is spiritual: these spiritual teachers you are talking about, or me, who is interested in how people live? You cannot talk about spiritual development to people who have to work 16 hours a day, for a dollar a day, to keep their family from starving. The crisis today is a spiritual one, but it is focused in the political and economic fields and can only be resolved in these fields.

Q. How can you combine this 'miracle' of the existence of Maitreya with man's free will?
A. You will find in practice that there is no contradiction. For the Masters, man's free will is sacrosanct and is never infringed by Them. The coming into the everyday world by Maitreya is not really a miracle. He does so under Law and according to plan, and His coming has been prepared for many years. It is simply that people, for the most part, have not heard of Him or the Plan.

Q. Provided that humanity has free will, how is it possible for Maitreya to intervene at a given time without infringing our free will? He said: "Whether they are ready or not, I am coming."
A. His coming, if undeclared as such, does not infringe our free will. I am afraid that the majority of people, even now, are unaware that Maitreya is in the world.

Q. Why not ask Maitreya to speak directly instead of always through you?
A. You do not keep a dog and bark yourself! The coming of a teacher of the stature of Maitreya has to be prepared for far in advance.

Q. If the Masters must wait for humanity to produce good karma before They can manifest Themselves openly, does this mean that They also are subject to karma?
A. The Masters do not make personal karma, but Their actions in relation to humanity are conditioned by world karma. Humanity does not have to 'produce good karma' but only to take the first steps themselves in the right direction.

Q. Realistically speaking, if Maitreya does appear, aren't there going to be people who will want to get rid of him? What then?
A. This problem does not arise. "Realistically speaking" there will be many people who will want to get rid of Him. There are people who always want to get rid of anyone who is doing good for the world – like Martin Luther King or President Kennedy; it always happens. Abraham Lincoln was assassinated because he had a vision of right relationships for humanity. They could try, but they would fail. How do you get rid of someone if you cannot even see Him, if He can disappear at will; Who is omniscient, omnipresent, Who has created a body and can recreate it a moment later?

Q. You say that the Master Jesus is near Rome. Do you mean geographically or does He belong to the Christian community, though unknown?
A. I mean geographically. The Master Jesus has lived in the outskirts of Rome for a number of years. He is not a member of the Christian community as such but has disciples in the Vatican through whom He works.

Q. You said that Prince Gautama was overshadowed by the Buddha. If so, it means that all his work of ascetism, meditation, detachment etc was given to him by a Master. Then this limits the possibility to reach 'knowledge' and spiritual experience. What is your point of view?

A. I have said that the Prince Gautama was overshadowed by the Buddha, but Gautama was already a fourth-degree initiate, so that all the qualities that you mention were already present in Him. What He gained by the overshadowing was the high spiritual status which has inspired millions for 2,600 years.

Q. What has happened to make the Masters return to the world now, after 98,000 years?

A. The Masters have for long known that They would return to the world. They have come to the end of a cycle in Their own evolution which requires Their return in group formation to show Their capacity to function simultaneously on all planes. The only question was when. The world has nuclear weapons; there are 28 countries which have atomic weapons of which only a fraction would be needed to destroy all life on Earth. So the Masters are coming forward with Maitreya (He announced His intention to return in 1945, at the end of World War II) to prevent destruction of all life on our planet. If allowed to go on as we are now we could destroy all life. The tensions inherent in the divisions between developed and developing countries have within them the seeds of world war, and that would be nuclear.

Q. Have the 14 Masters on Earth reincarnated or have they just appeared on Earth?

A. They are in Their own, adult, physical bodies and have emerged from Their retreats to take up Their positions in the modern world.

*Q. In **Share International** of March 1994 there was an article on the South Indian sage Sri Ganapathi Sachchidananda Swamiji who has his ashram in Mysore. He performs the same miracles as do Sai Baba and Swami Premananda, materializing vibhuti, lockets etc as also was mentioned in the article in **Share International**. On Mahashivaratri night Sri Ganapathi-ji also materializes shivalingams, but unlike Sai Baba and Swami Premananda not from his mouth but out of the fire during a fire ceremony. For this Swamiji enters the fire pit performing the ceremony for about half an hour without being hurt by the big flames. His disciples believe him to be the Avatar of the Hindu God Dattatreya, through whom the energies of Brahma, Vishnu and Shiva work. Can your Master explain how he fits into the circle of the Masters of the South Indian Lodge and his relationship with the other two great Avatars we know in South India, Sai Baba and Swami Premananda?*

A. Sri Ganapathi Sachchidananda Swamiji is one of a small group of Avatars Who have come into incarnation at this time of danger and change for humanity. The methods and approaches may vary but the underlying purpose is service to planet Earth.

*Q. In **The Reappearance of the Christ** by A.A. Bailey, it states: "It is the Physical Presence upon our planet of such recognized spiritual figures as the Lord of the World, the Ancient of Days; the seven Spirits Who are before the Throne of God; the Buddha, the spiritual leader of the East; and the Christ, the spiritual leader of the West – all of Whom are brought at this climaxing time to our attention." Does the word 'physical' in this context mean that: (1) Sanat Kumara is a man living on the planet as is the Lord Maitreya? (2) The seven Spirits are also manifesting in human form? (3) That the Buddha is actually in a human body and on our planet at this*

time? The paragraph certainly reads as if this is true.
A. (1) Yes. (2) Yes. (3) Apart from Maitreya, the Christ, all the above-named personages exist, in etheric physical bodies, on the highest centre, Shamballa.

WHAT SHOULD WE DO?

"Make known to all that I am here, that I am returned and prepare men for the Day of Declaration, the day of God's Gift; for on that day, men will celebrate together the achievement of God's Will. My Coming is nothing less." (Maitreya, from Message No. 25)

Q. I have read your information about Maitreya but I don't know how to 'give it a place' in my everyday life. I believe it, but it also seems unreal. Can you help?
A. Maitreya's coming is about world change: change in our understanding of the needs of the planet, the ecological balance; the change in our economic systems so that all people are fed and cared for properly; change in relationships between people everywhere. The true understanding that humanity is one will show the absolute necessity for this profound transformation. It is the making of a new world.

You are not alone on the planet and therefore you will see that these changes relate to you and your life, and this will give a deepening sense of the reality and meaning of Maitreya's coming.

Maitreya does not come alone but is head of a substantial group of perfected men, the Masters of Wisdom. As humanity takes seriously the advice and guidance of Maitreya and the Masters, there will begin this process of world change, which eventually will cover every aspect of our lives. This will of course affect you as it affects everyone else. Think about the coming of Maitreya in this way and I think you will get a deeper understanding of what His coming means to us.

Q. What should we do now that we have heard your information?

A. I myself am 100 per cent convinced because of my experiences over many years, but even if you are only 5 per cent sure – do what I am doing – make it known to the best of your ability – tell people, talk to the media, write articles, hold meetings! Tell everyone who will listen that this event is happening. Simply tell what you know, or what you believe.

If you are somewhat convinced (it doesn't matter if you do not know all the answers, just say you don't know), tell what you believe. In this way you are bearing witness and people will listen to you. They may not necessarily be convinced, but they hear the information. Their minds become more open to the possibility. That is the important thing.

Q. What can I do right now? I am only one small individual.

A. You are not just one person. You are one of millions all over the world; millions of right thinking people of goodwill. Join them. They, like you, want peace in the world and know that it is the injustices in the world that prevent peace. Make it known. Join with others, join groups.

Humanity is a tremendous force for good, and the changes will take place through the raised voice of the people. The voice of the people of all nations rising up, inspired by Maitreya, led by Him, activated by Maitreya – whether they know He is Maitreya or not. The united will of the people will force the governments to change.

Q. Will good triumph over evil?

A. Yes! Indeed. The end is known from the beginning. Good will inevitably triumph because it is the will of the divine Being Who ensouls this planet. But we have to make it so. It does not happen by itself. Maitreya puts it this way: "Nothing happens by itself. Man must act and implement his will." It does not matter what ideals we have, how much we would love everybody to be at peace, to have enough to eat, not to have millions starving, no little children with swollen bellies because they have had no food for weeks. None of that any more. It does not happen unless we act and make it so.

Q. If you are correct in thinking that the Christ and the Masters are in and coming into the world, is this not something altogether too big, too great an experience for ordinary people to deal with?

A. You will find that Maitreya and the Masters, although from our point of view perfected spiritual beings, are straightforward, simple, and totally respectful in their approach to humanity. They do not, and will not ever, behave like remote Gods of popular imagination. They are men, like us, but men without fault. They have a ready sense of humour, simplicity of approach, and They know better than we do ourselves the inner spiritual nature of all people. Maitreya is the Lord of Love; the Spiritual Hierarchy is the Centre in the planet in which the Love of God is expressed, and that exemplifies Their approach to us. It is unconditional.

Q. Can we tell anybody about your information and about Maitreya?

A. Anybody! Anybody who will listen to you! Even if you believe it only a tiny, little bit – tell it at that level. If you have complete conviction – make it known at that level. Tell others. In this way you create a climate of hope and expectation for His coming so that He can enter our lives without infringing our free will. That is the most important thing you could do today.

Q. What's the most important service we can do at this time in the world's history?

A. Make known the fact of Hierarchy's return to open work, and the presence and plans of Maitreya and the Masters.

Q. As the New Age starts, what simple changes can we make?
A. Implement sharing. Create justice and therefore peace. Create right human relations and therefore create unity and synthesis which is the key to the age of Aquarius. Realize that we are all One, brothers and sisters of one human society. All apparent differences are of no importance – whatever nationality or colour, these are not important. We have all probably had lives in different races, colours and nationalities. If you're Dutch now, who knows, you may be Chinese, African or Romanian in your next life. Make friends with them now!

Q. I am happy about having found your website and to learn about Maitreya and his teachings. It has allowed me to open my eyes and find a lot of answers to my questions. But there is something that I don't understand. Since I have read about Maitreya, I have become hyper-sensitive. Every time I see something sad or horrible on television, or even if I see an old woman walking down the streets or something beautiful, I start to cry. If somebody tells me his sorrows or pains I can feel it emotionally or even physically as if I am this person. I would like to know if I can do something about it, because I can't control it and I am starting to feel ridiculous in the eyes of my friends and people in general.

Since I have known about Maitreya, I have an inner conflict. I don't know how to incorporate Maitreya's teachings into my material life and into this material society. There is no day that ends without me thinking about the world's problems. It makes me apathetic and I feel guilty and useless. I know that you are not a psychologist, but if you could give me some advice, it would certainly help me.
A. This reaction is a brilliant expression of how a sensitive re-

sponse, even to the ideas, the thoughts and the inner meaning of Maitreya's words, opens the heart. That is what has happened in this case. The writer is responding (correctly) with what Maitreya calls "honesty of mind and sincerity of spirit" inherent in all of us, but unfortunately seldom so well displayed. It is an expression of the underlying oneness and unity of humanity. Maitreya, however, also advocates the development of detachment, I suppose what Buddhists call dispassion, the lack of which gives this individual such a difficult time. He/she can learn to experience vividly all the pain and suffering in the world. But when the decision is made to do something about it, to get involved in its cure, the first step in detachment can be taken. As doctors and nurses learn to deal with the most harrowing experiences without getting emotionally involved, their detachment allows them to carry out their necessary work. That is why Maitreya rates detachment so highly in the qualities to be acquired.

Maitreya Himself is omnipresent, experiences moment to moment the pain and suffering, the terrible, ongoing agony of millions throughout the world, yet is detached and filled with joy; otherwise He could not help them or carry out His mission.

Involvement in service is the ideal way to gain detachment. The writer might consider joining a Transmission Meditation group as a first step in that direction. If I may say so, I find this letter a beautiful and eminently correct response to the thoughts and ideas of Maitreya, the Lord of Love.

Q. I used to believe your information and hoped to see Maitreya all these years, but the story is getting harder and harder to believe. Why can't He just come into full public view now? Surely things in the world can't get much worse? Many people can't stand to hear or see the news any longer – there is too much suffering and too much wrong.

A. I can understand this feeling, but it is just a feeling and does not take into account the Law that Maitreya cannot ignore: that is the Law of human free will. At any time in the last 30 years, if we had ourselves taken some steps to right the wrongs of today, to implement the principle of sharing, to restore justice and peace to the world, then we would have seen Maitreya openly long ago. Blame ourselves and not Maitreya (or me!)

Q. I feel sad when the Masters of the world hide so well – we are ready for this, we are fed-up with every day's stupidity with the world, why can't they come forward now, more often for those who are ready?

A. This is part of the same idea – sit back and ask God or Masters to come and clean up our mess. We have to do it. We have to be responsible for the mess we are making. We cannot sit back and rely on God or the Masters to do it for us. If we do not want it, it will never happen. Humanity has free will – it is the greatest gift, the divinity in humanity. If we did not have free will we would not evolve. That free will is sacrosanct as far as the Masters are concerned, and They will never infringe it. So They cannot come out and clear up everything for us. They know it is not a lovely world for millions and millions of people. It is all right for well-nourished, well-heeled people in successful European countries, but there are millions of people starving to death who see their children dying because they have nothing to give them, because there is nothing for hundreds of miles in every direction – not even clean water to drink.

We are so complacent – Europeans, Americans, Japanese, in our comfortable little life (I know it is not comfortable for everybody, but in broad general terms) – we do not give a thought to how the vast majority lives and dies. If we do not see this we will never change it. If we want it to change we have to act – otherwise it does not happen.

Q. You have said that Maitreya knows we will make the right choices; it gives the impression that everything will be all right in the end, so why worry? But surely we have to make sacrifices and make an effort to change things? We need to be motivated to make changes.

A. Yes! Yes! Yes! Exactly. That is the whole point. *We* have to do it; we have to make the changes. As Maitreya says: "Nothing happens by itself. Man must act and implement his will." [Maitreya, from Message No. 31] We cannot just sit back and let somebody else do it. If we want change we have to do it – call for change, march, organize, do everything legal to bring our desire for change to the notice of those who can produce change. Here is an opportunity for anyone to lead the way, to call for change, start the European call for justice and freedom for all. Why don't you? Why come to listen to me? You could be out marching with banners calling for peace, justice and freedom in the world. That is the only way it will take place. It may be inspired by Maitreya; His energy will bring it into being. But we have to do it. We have to demand it.

The voice of the people is gaining ground – but you have to listen hard to hear it; we must make it louder. What Maitreya can do is educate, inform, inspire, create a reliable vehicle – the voice of the people of all countries of the world – and create an articulate mass against which no country in the world can stand. We need an informed, educated world public opinion for peace, justice and freedom. Nothing less will do. That is how it will be.

Q. How should we address Maitreya, for instance, if we want to 'talk' to Him or ask for His help?

A. Maitreya has given a simple, direct means of contacting Him. Use the 'Hand' of Maitreya which is given for this purpose. Simply look at it and that immediately draws His attention to the person asking for His help. [See the photograph of Maitreya's 'Hand' on page 114.]

Q. I am in a way quite surprised that your magazine gives so much importance to Maitreya's miracles. Not that I myself have the slightest doubt, but rather I think that speaking too much of the miracles may divert quite a few people from the path. In a way, my approach would tend to be of the following kind: "Oh, Lord, I do believe in you IN SPITE of your miracles." Or maybe it is the word 'miracle' itself that I cannot come to terms with. Because in fact what we call 'miracles' is something perfectly natural for the Lord Maitreya, and the most surprising thing about it is that we should be surprised. Could you comment?

A. The writer is not alone in his response to our reporting on miracles, but these are signs of Maitreya's presence and for many are a clear indication that His presence is a fact. Maitreya has said: "Those who search for signs will find them, but My method of manifestation is more simple." [Maitreya, from Message No. 10] For religious people they are a sign of hope, and many look for, and even demand, such miracles before they will accept and believe in the existence of the Teacher, by whatever name they know Him.

Q. Is it my imagination or is there an increasing number of patterns of light? They seem to be everywhere!

A. You are quite right. They are increasing so that they are now seen in almost every country in the world. [See examples of light patterns on pages 112-113.]

Q. There are many stories of people being healed by patterns of light which appear all around the world. Is their function one of healing?

A. The patterns of light are not healing lights per se, but from time to time Maitreya uses the light demonstration to perform the recorded 'miracle' healings.

Q. Maitreya seems to be appearing to people who know His identity, and they know that He knows that they know etc. Is this an indication that the Emergence has entered a new phase?

A. Yes. Maitreya is certainly appearing more, and more openly, to groups involved in the work of the Reappearance, even in guises already confirmed as being Him. It certainly gives the impression that His outer appearance is near, which I believe is the case.

Q. I have the impression that the Lord Maitreya is showing more of Himself, that is, appearing to people more frequently – still in a guise perhaps, but letting them see Him more as He really is? Is this the case?

A. No, this is not the case. In the guise of various 'familiars' He has sustained the same frequency of appearance for many years, but is appearing, as already stated, more frequently in a guise that has already been confirmed to be that of Maitreya.

Q. I read your website regularly. Please explain why the Masters spend Their valuable time to appear to someone – to stay sometimes for an hour or two with people who work with you – when They are so busy and there are so many problems in the world, so many people to heal, rescue and comfort. It doesn't seem logical.

A. The answer lies in the fact that when Maitreya or a Master appears to someone, it is not the Master or Maitreya the person sees and talks with but a 'familiar', a thoughtform, which He can invest with some fragment of His consciousness. The mastery of a Master involves being able to divide His consciousness into thousands of separate and simultaneous activities. In Maitreya's case, He is literally omnipresent.

Q. Once Maitreya is in the world and we start to take action, will our actions be potentized or made more effective by Him?

A. Maitreya is in the world, but once He emerges openly, every action that we take in the right direction – that is towards oneness, justice, freedom for all people – will invoke His help and energy. He will potentize our actions and the changes will proceed with enormous speed and order.

*Q. (1) How many people have heard the information about Maitreya? (2) Out of those, how many are open to the possibility of it? (3) How many people actually believe it? (**Share International**, September 2004)*
A. (1) About 30 million. (2) About 20 million. (3) About 2 million.

Q. (1) Approximately how many people, as part of their soul purpose, have come into incarnation at this time to help prepare the way for Maitreya and the Hierarchy? (2) Of this number, what percentage have responded to this call and are actually involved in this process?
A. (1) 4,600. (2) 70 per cent.

Q. Why is it so important to be incarnated at this time?
A. This is a unique time in the history of the Earth. A new cosmic cycle – the age of Aquarius – is just beginning; consequently, enormous changes in every area of life will take place over the next 2,350 years or so. Above all, a great change in human consciousness will gradually unfold, greater by far in depth and range than at any previous point in history. This will be the result of the extraordinary stimulus given to our evolution by the energies of Aquarius and by the externalization of the work of our Spiritual Hierarchy for the first time in 98,000 years. The Christ, the Lord Maitreya, and a large group of His disciples will be physically present for the whole of the Age, aiding humanity to evolve in peace, freedom and justice.

An extraordinary opportunity is thus provided to everyone

to serve the world, helping to create the new structures in whatever department of life calls you. Who would not want to be around at such a time?

Q. What difference do you think it makes in a person's life if they believe in reincarnation or not?
A. It is obvious, is it not, that if you 'believe', even as an intellectual idea, that you will live again and again, it removes one of the great fears of life, namely, the fear of death. It gives you a sense of proportion and 'lawfulness' in this life and relates you, inevitably, to the Law of Karma (of cause and effect), the basic law governing our existence on Earth.

Q. Could you please elaborate on our being incarnated specifically to be involved in the Reappearance work? Have all of us here (at this conference) incarnated now for this purpose?
A. Maitreya puts it so clearly and yet you doubt Him [see Maitreya's Message No. 7]. You want me to elaborate on it? It is either true or it is not true. What could I say that would add one iota to that and strengthen your conviction? You talk about trust. Trust is the result of conviction, and the conviction is the result of trust. You have to have the conviction. You have to have the trust. You also have to have the experience.

If Maitreya tells you that this group was brought into the world in order to do this work, you can believe it or not. It is obvious that if you ask me to elaborate on this that you do not believe it. You do not really have the conviction that this is true and, therefore, you do not do much. I am not talking about everybody, but I would say the majority of people in this room now do not do very much except to 'work on themselves', which is not very much. You cannot have it both ways.

Everybody wants to be seen, recognized, treated as a disciple. Disciple means discipline. That is where the word comes from: one who is disciplined. If you are not disciplined, if you

83

are not working, if you are not serving, you are not doing the work of making known this information in every way you can, as often as you can, spending time and energy, then you are not doing it because you do not believe it. Maitreya has said you have come into the world to do this work. Somebody has to do it; do you understand? Someone has to do it.

When Maitreya called a Conference in London in April 1990 He was living in one of the temples (not the same temple as He is in now), and He asked the swamis to write out invitations to the Conference. About 350 people were invited and maybe half to two-thirds of them came. They were all powerful people in the world: kings, politicians and journalists, economists and businessmen, religious leaders, etc. There were all kinds of people, all people with a fair amount of sensitivity, certainly intelligence, some with much more than that. But the swamis would not write out the invitation cards. So who do you think did it? Maitreya. Maitreya, the World Teacher and head of Hierarchy, the Embodiment of Love, wrote by hand the invitation cards. He said: someone has to do it. He would not use force or even raise His voice to the swamis; He just said: somebody has to do it. But they would not engage in that kind of thing. They were too into their religion, and so Maitreya, Who is not into religion, wrote out the cards.

Somebody has to do it. Somebody has to make this information known. It does not happen by itself. As Maitreya says: "Man must act and implement his will." You have to do it. You just cannot leave it to other people. That is complacency – leaving it to other people to do.

I cannot prove to you that you are in the world now, incarnated for this reason. I cannot tell you if you have come into incarnation to do this work. But if Maitreya, Who is talking to the group, says you have come into the world to do this, then I believe it. I do not know about you. You do not have to believe Him. Nobody is asking you to believe Him. You can only believe Him or not believe Him. You have to do it from yourself, not because He asks you to believe Him or I ask you to believe Him. I do not care whether you believe Him or not.

You either believe this to be true, or not, that the One Who said it was Maitreya, that those words came from the mind of Maitreya and He uttered them (through me to be sure), but He uttered them and I believe that they are true. I believe that you have come into the world to do this work. That you are not doing it very strongly I also believe to be true, but maybe I am prejudiced. Maybe I expect too much. I think that Maitreya probably expects less than I do, because He knows you better than I do.

But so little goes a long way. You would be surprised. So little work goes a long way, has an effect that you cannot see. You talk about this story. This is the greatest story in the world. There is nothing that has ever been said that is more important and more enlightening than this story. That is not because of me. I am only doing my part of the job. It is the most important event in the history of the world so far. Enormous things will come out of this, the whole transformation of the world, a transformation in ways which you cannot even dream about, cannot imagine with all our science fiction behind you. You cannot imagine how the world will be in 25 years' time.

So I believe when Maitreya says you have come into the world to do this work, I believe He means this truly, precisely, simply. You have come into the world to do this work. Well, do it. Simple as that. Do it!

Q. If Maitreya intends making use of an opportunity to appear on television fairly soon, what would be most useful for the groups to focus on at fairs and lectures and in publicity material? Presumably Maitreya will be making the case for sharing as the only lasting solution to injustice and terrorism. If that is correct then would you advise that we focus on His social con-

cerns and, above all, sharing as a key?
A. Yes, and the urgency of making the information known.

*Q. The **Share International** photo exhibition sounds like a great approach to the public. The photo panels may not necessarily talk about Maitreya's emergence but they show the problems of the world, educate people and show Maitreya's priorities. Would you also recommend this approach highly?*
A. I would certainly recommend this approach. I think it is a great idea, one of many ways of approaching the public. It is common sense. It would also promote *Share International* magazine, and it is simple. The simplicity is the keynote. You look at the back covers of a magazine, and they draw attention to the front cover or the middle pages. If it is all like this, you might think, then it is a very interesting magazine.

Maitreya, Himself, dressed as a photo journalist, looked at this exhibition in Japan very intently for about two hours. Then He commended it many times. He said if many people showed those photographs around the world, it would very quickly have an effect in pointing people in the direction of justice. I think it is obvious that if you show such pictures in context with the Reappearance story, people will grasp what it is about. [See article by Michiko Ishikawa 'Maitreya visits SI Photo Exhibit', *Share International*, July/August 2000.]

Q. Will one of Maitreya's tasks be to open our hearts to others' suffering, and does the photo exhibition serve that purpose?
A. Certainly one of Maitreya's hopes is to open our hearts to others' suffering. That is what He does every time He releases His energies into the world. It has been at the centre of everything He has said and everything I have said in all the talks and writings I have done. That is exactly what He hopes to do, to open our hearts to the world's suffering. That way you change the world. He said: "Take your brother's need as the

measure for your action and solve the problems of the world. ✗
There is no other course." [Maitreya, from Message No. 52]
He spells it out. Does the photo exhibition serve that purpose?
It could go some way to doing that.

Q. Could you talk about the nature of love and consciousness?
A. What I am talking about is the manifestation of love. Love
is not something which conjures up a lovely feeling, and we
put our hands over the heart and say: "I am filled with love.
Oh, I do love my wife, my children and my grandparents and
the people in my community. But I do not like these Muslims.
I hate these Muslims. They are behind 9/11, I am sure of it. I
hate them." That is love as we know love.

Love is nothing to do with that. Love is an action. It is an
ability to act according to the needs of humanity. You have to
learn to love the world. To love yourself is easy. To love your
wife and your children is easy, your own community is easy,
your own nation is, (it is getting difficult for America), but it
is relatively easy. To learn to love the world as a whole, to see
all people as one and to respect everybody, with a right to what
the world has to give, that is love. Love in action is what
counts.

*Q. Why do you tantalize people with the hope and expectation
that the answers to the world's problems will come from outside themselves? Any peace that is imposed from without, even
by God himself, will eventually be seen as only another form
of tyranny. True peace must first be planted as a seed in individual human hearts, then nourished and cultivated until it is
finally established. Only then will it be able to grow to matu-
rity, and delight the world with its long-desired and
much-anticipated fruits.*
A. I quite agree – and that is what has been taking place over
the last 30-odd years.

Q. Has there been any change in humanity's consciousness since your first US lecture that might let the Christ come forward more openly?

A. Yes, despite appearances, humanity is awakening to its problems and, to some extent, their solutions. From the point of view of Hierarchy, real progress has been made.

Q. Why do the people feel the new energies but the politicians don't? They're people too.

A. Yes, but the politicians are interested in power; they all want to handle power. Power is an energy and like all energies can be used wisely or unwisely. Some politicians use power unwisely and cause various crises. Their time is coming to an end. The most important and powerful structure in the future will be a truly educated, spiritually oriented and aware world public opinion. The people will truly inherit the Earth.

Maitreya also comes for the politicians, but He comes especially for the people. The politicians are so selfish, powerful and greedy that they can look after themselves. And they usually do!

Q. Please explain why we in America are such an important part of Maitreya's work? Can we really make a huge contribution?

A. Because America is so large, so rich, so aggressive and, therefore, so influential, that it has a huge impact on the direction being taken by humanity. This can be for good or for ill. The present administration [the Bush administration] in the US is bent on a very destructive course which could be disastrous for the world and so needs very careful handling, and a clear understanding of its motives and of the forces which drive it.

Q. Sai Baba is asking his followers to organize public meetings to spread the word about him. This is new. Is he helping raise people's consciousness to be open to Maitreya's message?

A. Yes.

Q. Will the daily recitation of The Great Invocation speed the coming of Maitreya?
A. Yes, and the emergence of those Masters Who are planned to externalize Their work. [See The Great Invocation on page 118]

MESSAGE FROM MAITREYA

"My dear friends. I am close to you now.

Many of you have awaited My presence for a long time. I am about to step forward openly before all men, and to begin my outer mission.

There is no distance between us. Know this. Understand this.

When you ask Me through the 'hand' or directly to Me for help, that help, you should know, is assured. It is possible that you will not recognize that the help has been given, but so it will be. Trust Me to aid you, for it is to do so that I come.

I shall exhort you to work with Me for the good of all.

This is the opportunity to grow quicker, faster than you have ever done before, and so bring you to the Feet of That One Whom we call God.

Be not afraid of the many problems which arise now almost daily in the world.

These events are transient and soon men will come to understand that they have before them a future bathed in light.

So will it be."

[This message was given by Maitreya, telepathically through Benjamin Creme, on 27 September 2007, at the end of his interview for a television documentary at the Share Nederland Information Centre in Amsterdam, the Netherlands.]

STUDY AND PRACTICE OF THE TEACHINGS

"Soon will you see Me in full vision and, as you do, realize that for many this meeting is not the first. Many of you have served Me before, long, long ago, and, coming now into the world, stand ready once again. Know this, My friends, and seize the opportunity now offered to serve Me and the world." (Maitreya, from Message No. 88)

Q. Benjamin Creme's Master urges us to do systematic study of the teachings. As far as studying goes, how can we avoid the danger of having too much information and not integrating it, having spiritual indigestion? Is there any practical way to avoid this?

A. The way to avoid spiritual indigestion and to make best use of the information that you are learning, is to practise it. For it to have any value in your life you have to put it into effect, actually practise the teachings.

The precepts are given to set the ground plan for the correct use of the teachings. There are people who know the Alice Bailey teachings like some people know the Bible, chapter and verse. They could quote almost any page of the books by heart. But they do not necessarily live the teachings, except to a limited extent. It is to them like an academic body of knowledge, which has its value, but it is not a major value. You could know nothing about the teachings, but actually live them daily. This science is also not something you can read up in a book and apply; it is not applied science in that sense. It is a science which is also an art. It is an understanding of the nature of the universe, which is an understanding of the nature of life.

You can only understand life in the macro-cosmic sense if you have experienced it in the microcosm. As above, so below. You can know what the greater is if you experience it in you, the smaller, because there is only one life. Life manifests as solar systems and also as the human being. It is exactly the same life. That is why Sai Baba can say: "Yes, I am God. But you, too, are God. There is only God; that is all there is, so how could you be other than God?" The difference is, of course, that He knows He is God and, what is more important, He demonstrates it, while we do not. We do not know it and do not demonstrate it. Even if we knew it, theoretically, we would not necessarily demonstrate it. You have to know it in the sense of 'being' it to demonstrate it.

To invoke the intuition, you have to fill out the requirements of the lower mind. So these teachings are given in a particular way, and they are difficult. They are not made difficult expressly, but they are difficult because the Master DK had the task of bringing down His intuitive, Buddhic, knowledge of all that He is talking about to a level where it will mean something to our lower concrete mind – and invoke our intuition. To say you understand the teachings by intuition means that the soul is involved. By invoking the intuition, which comes from the soul, you are making contact with the soul. The more the teachings become an everyday part of your consciousness, not something that you have to look up, but to do with everyday reality, the more the intuition will flow, the more your intuitive understanding of the teachings will occur. If your intuitive understanding is such, so will your life be. That radiates outward, because it is the nature of the soul to radiate. As that becomes part of your everyday, living awareness, it radiates out and communicates. Then you get the creativity of the disciple. It is not something just to look up in a book. You can do that for ever.

Q. As far as priorities for studying are concerned, should we start with Maitreya's teachings, the Alice Bailey books, or Benjamin Creme's books?

A. I would say, because they are the simplest and the most direct, and the closest to you, the teachings of Maitreya in so far as they have been given out through His associate. [See *Maitreya's Teachings: The Laws of Life*.] That is the first step. They are perhaps the most difficult but the most easy of access, because this is how Maitreya will talk to the world, bringing it down to the very simplest level. He will be talking to the whole world, which has to change in consciousness. He is not going to say: "Do this meditation or that meditation, then align this chakra with that chakra, then build the bridge", and so on. He will not do anything of that at all.

He will talk about honesty of mind, sincerity of spirit, and detachment. These are the three. He gives them as three very potent forces of evolution. They are potent because they are the essentials. They are the essentials because only in growing detachment can you advance to the point of being a Master, of being Self-realized. Only through honesty of mind and sincerity of spirit can you become detached. Unless you become detached, you cannot do the others. Unless you do the others, you cannot become detached.

Life is really about detachment. Without detachment, you cannot make one step forward in evolution. A growing detachment, by its very nature, frees you from identification with your body, your emotions, your mental concepts. That is how the steps are taken. I would say, read Maitreya's teachings and put them into practice. Read Krishnamurti and put it into practice. It is not simply a question of reading and knowing; it is a question of putting it into practice. They are talking about exactly the same thing, the same process – detachment.

Q. There is a 'healthy debate' going on within some Transmission Meditation groups: some think it is very important to meet for study groups and 'esoteric discussion groups' while others think that the situation in the world and the day-

to-day work of informing the public, etc, needs their attention at this particular time. Could you please comment and advise?
A. This is a time of crisis and tension and requires the fixed attention and application of all the groups working for the Reappearance. Some groups have 'relapsed' into the glamour of 'self-education study groups' at the expense of informing the public about Maitreya and His plans. They seem to have decided that Maitreya's emergence is years away so that there is no special hurry to inform the public. They are wrong – and will be found wanting.

Q. Where to start? Working on ourselves first or spreading our information about the presence of Maitreya and the Masters and Maitreya's priorities?
A. 'Working on oneself' would depend upon your approach. It may mean total focus of one's attention on oneself, and by so doing, thinking you are working on yourself.

What does it mean: to work on yourself? Working on yourself means taking responsibility. You work on yourself to improve your character, and you recognize people by the quality of their character. The more advanced, the more evolved a person is, the more profound will be the nature of their thought, the more dependable, the more creative, they will be. These are all characteristics of accepting the responsibility of life.

So, to 'develop' oneself, to devote one's attention to oneself and therefore to 'work' on oneself, usually does not mean anything at all. It is often just a way of not doing anything, not paying attention to the outer world, not telling the world that Maitreya and a group of Masters are in the world, not telling the world about Maitreya's priorities and the need for change. You have no time to do that if you are 'working on yourself' in that way.

You do not work on yourselves separately from telling the world about Maitreya. You can do both at the same time. If you are really telling the world about Maitreya, you are working on yourself. You may not see it in these terms but you are actually doing so. You cannot go on a stage and talk to 50 or 500 people about the coming of Maitreya and His group of Masters and what it means for humanity, the significance, the results of it, the actions of humanity in relation to it (because these are crucial) without being changed. You have to think, put these words together, say them to the world. That is working on yourself. It is not a separate thing that you could do instead of talking about Maitreya's priorities. You cannot talk about Maitreya's priorities without simultaneously working on yourself.

Working on yourself for most students of the esoteric teachings is to read Alice Bailey: to read it day in and day out, to always have a volume under an arm ready to whip out every time they have a coffee, and to sit for hours in the coffee bar, reading occasionally, and looking around and thinking about it, 'working on themselves'. That is what many people do. It is so useless. The Alice Bailey books are wonderful and should be read diligently, but they are only books, and are meant to stimulate action as well as thought.

Working on yourself is action. It is work, actual work, getting on a stage, getting over your nervousness, your stage fright, opening your mouth and talking to other people, just one person, half a dozen, half a dozen hundred, it does not matter. The same effort is taken to talk to two people as is taken in talking to 200 people. You say the same words. You are lucky if 200 hear it instead of two, but you have to start somewhere.

I remember when I started. Sometimes there would be four people in the audience and all four would have heard the story before! It is not easy in the beginning, but you just have to have a bit of courage. To have courage you have to work on yourself by getting to know the story, what it is you want to say, thinking about it. I do not mean learning it by rote, but seeing how you can best express it. That is working to get ready to present it to people. The presenting of it is working on yourself. You grow as you do it.

You work on yourself in order to grow, and the best way to grow is to grow in life. Do a service in the world and you grow. You cannot help it. By staying at home reading books, you are not really working on yourself. That is the way out. You will never go forward if you just rely on books, even the Alice Bailey books.

People do not read the books correctly anyway, and they read far too many, even of mine. (No, you cannot read too many of my books, that was just a slip of the tongue!) But if you read them correctly, you will hear me say in the books exactly what I am saying now. You change by doing things – really working on yourself. It is not a separate activity from telling the world about Maitreya. If you say what is the most important thing to you, well, the coming of Maitreya. He is the Christ. He is a great Avatar. He has come to change the world through you. How can He change the world through you if you are just 'working on yourself' by having coffee in the meantime, reading Alice Bailey?

Q. You say complacency is the root of all problems. How should we deal with complacency in ourselves and others?
A. You can only deal with complacency in yourself; get rid of it. It is a fault in character, a sense of separation which we must try to overcome. In others, all you can do is persuade; speak out, if it is a complacency that strongly affects the world as a whole. If it is on a much smaller scale, an individual thing, because there must be few people who are not complacent to some degree, we have to leave them to get over their own complacency.

It is a profound glamour as a result of ignorance of the fact that there is no separation in the world. There is no separation between the smallest atom and every other atom in the whole of the manifested universe. Every soul, and every one of us is a soul in incarnation, is related to every other soul in Cosmos.

So all you can do is deal with your own complacency, if you recognize it. If you do not recognize it then you cannot be free, you cannot help the world because you can be too complacent even to see the needs. Maitreya calls complacency, not money, 'the source of all evil'. Money is simply an impersonal energy, and energies can be used for good or for ill. You can use it for good on a broad, general scale, or you can hoard it and try to increase it for yourself and to pass on to your children and hope that they will pass it on to theirs.

It is all a big glamour caused by fear; because people are afraid they become complacent. They are too afraid to face the responsibilities and the true purpose and meaning of life, so they become complacent. They forget about other people. They do not think that they are in any way connected with people across the seas, people they do not know with different coloured skins and different religions.

That is what makes people complacent. It is a convenience. Complacency takes you out of your true human responsibility. You come into incarnation as a responsible Being. The baby is more responsible, initially, than the complacent adult. Babies come in as souls; they come in with a purpose, usually several purposes, and the fundamental purpose: the creation of right human relationships.

The soul cannot create right human relationship if its reflection, the personality, is complacent. Complacency is simply a way of sitting back and making no effort to include the world; and you can only do that when you have amassed a little money, a little bit of comfort, a little 'security'. Then you can bathe yourself in this and hope that the world will go away and leave you alone and not trouble you. Complacency is not wanting to be troubled by knowing of others who are pitifully worse off than oneself.

Q. We talked about trust and knowing that all will be well. Some comments were made about complacency slipping in. Please can you comment on the balance of trust, yet having to do the work?

A. Trust is nothing to do with complacency. Complacency is the result of fear. Trust is the result of conviction; that conviction of trust that you know what is, that your soul is telling you that this is true, that this is believable, that you can trust this. Maitreya or the Master says: "Have trust, all will be well, all manner of things will be well." They do not, however, expect you to sit back, therefore, and do nothing, become complacent.

You have to understand what trust is. Trust is a conviction. It is a conviction that this will be so, that all will be well, for example, and in time it will. Does that mean to say that in the meantime you just sit back and become complacent and say: "Well, I do not mind, it does not matter to me that there are millions starving in the world or a tiny fraction of people know about Maitreya, and I could do something to make that more, but what is the point? All will be well." That is complacency, but it is not trust. They are different.

When a Master says "All will be well", He means that and says it to remove fear. Fear prevents action, and if you have the conviction that all will be well you can work free from the fear which inhibits your action. It does not mean that you don't have to act at all, on the contrary. The more you have trust and are free from fear, the more useful and large in scope can be your action.

Trust and complacency are miles apart. If you have trust, you cannot be complacent. If you are complacent, then you do not have trust.

Q. Could you elaborate on the question of how the gap will be bridged between 'ordinary' people and the disciples in the world, from Creme's Master's article 'Step by Step' in the

*October 2007 issue of **Share International**?*

A. What the Master meant in connection with this is that because Maitreya and the Masters will be working openly in the world – teaching, answering questions from media and so on, teaching 'ordinary' people who come to meetings, who watch radio and television – They will give people an understanding of the simpler fundamental aspects of the Ageless Wisdom Teachings, and in so doing They will narrow the gap that now exists between the average man and woman in the street who does not read Alice Bailey or Blavatsky, and people who do.

At the moment, there is a gap between those who have read, to some extent, the esoteric teachings and the 'ordinary' people who have not. This makes it difficult for those disciples to speak and be understood by the average man in the street. The attempt is to narrow this gap by an approach by the Masters Themselves, on a relatively simple level, to this activity which has been done up till now by the disciples. To my mind it is a very welcome shift in the acquaintance of humanity in general with the esoteric laws, which are the very basis of our life.

Today, the average man or woman in the street (because of the influence of the 5th ray perhaps), in modern western civilization, is inclined not to recognize or accept the existence of anything that lies above the dense-physical plane. But if you are a student of the Ageless Wisdom teaching then you know that that is the starting point, the basic point, that everything is relative and that there is no end to that relativity. So there is an ever-expanding consciousness of what is.

Now, in order to bridge the gap between the man in the street and the average student of the Ageless Wisdom Teachings, the Masters are approaching the populace directly, Themselves, with some of the basic esoteric teachings. This will inevitably form a bridge, narrow the gap, between those who have read these teachings and who are working to some extent with these teachings, and those who have not.

THE EXPECTED EVENTS

PRESENT AND NEAR FUTURE

*Q. There is an extraordinary passage in **The Rays and the Initiations, Part Two**, by Alice A. Bailey, which was written in 1947 but seems to speak very much to present world conditions. The Master DK says: "The tension in the world today, particularly in the Hierarchy, is such that it will produce another and perhaps ultimate world crisis, or else such a speeding up of the spiritual life of the planet that the coming in of the long looked-for New Age conditions will be amazingly hastened.... The selfishness of the United States is also due to youth, but it will eventually yield to experience and to suffering; there is – fortunately for the soul of this great people – much suffering in store for the United States.... In the hands of the United States, Great Britain and Russia, and also in the hands of France, lies the destiny of the world disciple, Humanity. Humanity has been passing through the tests which are preparatory to the first initiation; they have been hard and cruel and are not yet entirely over. The Lords of Karma (four in number) are today working through these four Great Powers; it is, however, a karma which seeks to liberate, as does all karma. In the coming crisis, true vision and a new freedom, plus a wider spiritual horizon may be attained. The crisis, if rightly handled, need not again reach the ultimate horror.... the Jews [Editor: ie Zionists] have partially again opened the door to the Forces of Evil, which worked originally through Hitler and his evil gang. The 'sealing' of that door had not been successfully accomplished, and it is the part of wisdom to discover this in time. These Forces of Evil work through a triangle of evil, one point of which is to be found in the Zionist Movement in the United States, another in central Europe, and the third in Palestine [Editor: now Israel].... In the maps which are to be found in the Archives of the spiritual*

Hierarchy, the entire area of the Near East and Europe – Greece, Yugoslavia, Turkey, Palestine, the Arab States, Egypt and Russia – are under a heavy overshadowing cloud. Can that cloud be dissipated by the right thinking and planning of Great Britain, the United States and the majority of the United Nations or – must it break in disaster over the world?" (pp 428-430)

(1) Does this "ultimate world crisis" still lie ahead, (2) are we now in it or its early stages, or (3) has it been mitigated by the rapid evolutionary changes during the past half-century?
A. (1) No. (2) We are in its early stages. (3) It has been mitigated to some extent.

Q. (1) Was the "coming crisis" the Cold War and its nuclear threat? (2) Could it also be the world's present economic crisis?
A. (1) Yes. (2) Yes.

Q. (1) Does the "suffering in store for the United States" refer to remorse for the Iraqi War and/or (2) other military adventures, or (3) the effects of an economic crash?
A. (1) Not remorse but the effects of unilateral action and rejection of the rule of law of the United Nations. (2) Yes. (3) Yes.

Q. Every day more evidence comes to light of the United States, through agencies such as the CIA, bullying other countries and manipulating their sovereign affairs (such as elections) to benefit the US. (1) Has this always gone on, and we are now seeing the corruption come to the surface, as Maitreya predicted? Or (2) has the present US administration taken political corruption to new depths?
A. The United States is a young country, dominated as a personality by the lower aspects of the 6th ray of Idealism or Devotion. It therefore suffers from all of the vices of the ray:

devotion to its own interests, suspicion of others' motives, combativeness and self-assertion, self-deception about its own motives, etc, etc. Thus its bullying tactics are endemic and long-standing. Its inhabitants and governments believe they are spreading Freedom and Justice around the world, while they are actually serving their own interests. This self-deception is one of the chief characteristics of the ray. This political corruption has, therefore, always gone on; this administration, led by fundamentalist extremists, is simply taking it to new depths. The world, as the Master Djwhal Khul has written through Alice Bailey, is waiting for the 2nd-ray soul of America to express itself, as it did through the Marshall Plan after World War II.

*Q. In **Share International** Maitreya is said to have referred to "difficult times" ahead. What was He referring to? Did He mean the world situation now?*
A. He meant economic difficulties.

Q. I was shocked to hear you mention Israel as a point of evil. What's that about?
A. I am surprised the questioner was shocked, given the callous oppression of the Palestinian people by Israel. Israel justifies its action as part of the 'war on terrorism' as advocated by Mr Bush, who attacked Iraq, which was not terrorist and certainly not a threat to the US. After the defeat of the Axis powers by the Allies in 1945, the 'forces of evil', as we call them – 'the Lords of Materiality' as they are known by the Hierarchy of Light – were being gradually sealed off to their own domain: the upholding of the Matter aspect of the planet. With the creation of the state of Israel in 1948, by terrorist action against the British Mandatory Power and the people of Palestine, it was, according to the Master DK, "as if the forces of evil got a foot in the door again". Israel is the central point of a trian-

gle of evil which works through Israel, the Pentagon in the US and certain states in Eastern Europe.

What we are witnessing now is an explosion of this evil force which must be countered and resolved by humanity with the aid of the Hierarchy of Light – Maitreya and His group of Masters of the Wisdom.

*Q. There is an interesting passage in Alice Bailey's book **The Externalisation of the Hierarchy**. Alice Bailey refers to "the adjuster of finances", an advanced disciple of the Spiritual Hierarchy who will become active after the principle of barter and exchange (ie sharing) has begun to be adopted by the world. (1) Does this refer to an adjustment of the global marketplace, the global monetary system, or both? (2) Is the "adjuster of finances" actively working today? (3) Will the adjuster be working through the United Nations? (4) Will the adjuster be in charge of a special council or agency created by the international community for the express purpose of making this adjustment?*
A. (1) Both. (2) No. (3) Yes. (4) Yes.

Q. Please comment on the importance of publicly-owned land and facilities particularly in urban areas in the future – and particularly as related to Maitreya's priorities and the art of living.
A. All cities need publicly-owned land free from buildings or many buildings. One of Maitreya's future priorities, which my Master has written about, is the beautification of our cities. That must include the creation of far more parkland than most cities have today, for leisure, for recreation, for simply sitting in the sun and watching the butterflies – or land for the temples or objects of force that will be built in certain open spaces which will create equilibrium and residual energy for that area of the town or city. It is the study, therefore, of the energetic

properties of forms like the tetrahedron or pyramid, which have energetic properties simply because of their shape. Shape power is another term for that. There are many shapes of power which, when aligned, will be used to change the climate and benefit the air quality of cities throughout the globe.

Q. What kind of future do you see for America and the world within the next couple of decades?
A. If enough people accept quickly the changes that Maitreya will be calling for, we can transform life in America and the rest of the world very soon. Once the ideas of sharing and justice engage the imagination and are seen as the only ways to create peace and an end of terrorism and war, then millions will join the ranks around Maitreya.

You have no idea how eloquent Maitreya is, how simple and knowledgeable, with a mind which is razor sharp and can illumine every problem. His love and wisdom are endless, the love of God and the wisdom of all the ages. His ability to enter into the hearts of all and release His energy of love is the sword which He wields to change the world. The Sword of Cleavage is the energy of Love.

As people respond to this energy, the world will be divided – those who are clamouring for change along the lines Maitreya is advocating, and those who are fearful and looking to the past, who see Him as the antichrist, are fearful and do not know what to do. They will stand aside and watch the events, and so lose the opportunity presented, for the first time in history, to take part in the transformation of the world. It is up to each individual, from where he or she stands, to assert their divinity.

Maitreya is speaking about sharing, justice, freedom and right relationship. They are all divine principles. Freedom, justice and right relationship are at the basis of life and make for correct relationship between peoples and between nation and nation.

It is competition that leads to war and prevents right human relationship from evolving. The creation of correct human relationship is the next step forward in our evolution. When you have that you have the beginning of true divine life. The first step into sharing, says Maitreya, is the first step into your divinity. What could be simpler or truer?

Q. It is wonderful that light is slowly beginning to dawn on this planet despite the problems we still face. My question is: I constantly hear from various sources of impending disasters, calamities, and all sorts of doom and gloom about to take place on this planet, mostly by some interstellar object or forces within the Earth itself. Are we to expect a pole shift or a planetary object to collide with the Earth, or are these claims just fear-mongering by those who are easily influenced by the black lodge?

A. These predictions of gloom and doom are largely the product of fear-mongering by all and sundry when they are not the deliberate creations of those nefarious forces who seek always to keep humanity enthralled. There will indeed be climatic change, upheaval and difficulties in many parts of the world, but not the exaggerated portents of catastrophe and disaster.

It would almost seem that we cannot get enough of disaster to satisfy the emotional requirements of some people. The media play a huge part in the dissemination of this catastrophe syndrome by their sensational reportage. It must be good for the sale of newspapers and magazines. Change is always difficult for people, whether it is small changes or large changes. Changes of the kind which are transforming the world are particularly frightening for many people. What they do not know is the power of Maitreya the Christ and World Teacher, Who is now physically present among us, together with a large group of His disciples. Their energies are inspiring the best of humanity into realizing and implementing these changes. As

Maitreya said: "Have no fear. The end is known from the beginning. All will be well. All manner of things will be well."

Q. Does Maitreya think we will still change the world even if we are selfish and competitive?
A. Yes. Not everybody is selfish and competitive. Probably the majority of people are partly selfish and partly altruistic; people are mixed, not one hundred per cent this or that. There are degrees of selfishness and altruism. There is a great body of people who are ready for an unselfish action, ready to see justice in the world and therefore sharing.

Way back in 1924, in the Agni Yoga books, Maitreya said there had been a time when 10 true men could save the world. Then came a time when 10,000 was not enough. He will call on one billion.

About five or six years ago I asked my Master whether Maitreya had His one billion yet. Yes, I was told, Maitreya had 1.5 billion people He could call on. So it was 1.5 billion people out of 6.5 billion in the world whom He knew to be of goodwill, altruistic and ready to see new structures and new ways of living. Now (as of 2006), there are 1.8 billion people He can call on – more than enough.

Besides, we have no alternative. If I offer you life or death – what are you going to take? Maitreya will say: "You have a choice. Choose life, if you are sensible, and create a brilliant, golden, civilization, better than anything the world has ever seen. Or face annihilation." Which are you going to choose?

There has never been an Avatar, a Teacher, of such potency as Maitreya. Have no fear. The world will change quickly from being greedy and selfish to showing the true quality of humanity.

From Maitreya's point of view humanity is wonderful. Maitreya loves humanity. This is not only because He is the Lord of Love – that is why He is able to love humanity – despite everything, despite all our greed and selfishness. But He also sees the light of divinity in humanity. He is the head of the kingdom of souls. He sees the soul of humanity, and that soul is in every single human being. No matter how selfish or hateful we might seem, He sees that light of divinity in us, and on that you can rely.

MESSAGE FROM MAITREYA

"My friends, I am nearer to you than you may think. My heart beats step by step with yours. My heart cries for the suffering of so many. Yet I know that the hearts of those who hear Me now are open and willing to help. Fear not My friends. Give bravely and willingly to help all in need. When you do this you enter that area of divinity from which you come. This is the action of divinity itself.

So My friends, wait no longer for the manifestation of the great changes which are to come. Bring them about by your actions.

Think widely. Think that your brothers and sisters are yourselves, the same throughout the world. Do this My friends and see Me very soon.

My heart embraces you all."

*[This message was given by Maitreya, telepathically through Benjamin Creme, at the end of his interview on **Radio Ici & Maintenant**, in Paris, France, on 6 April 2006.]*

THE FIRST STEPS

by the Master —, through Benjamin Creme

When Maitreya appears before the world people will realize that they have known Him from before, and that His teaching is not strange or beyond their level of thought. Simple, indeed, will He be that all may understand.

Precisely His simplicity will astound. Nevertheless it will be found also that most people will experience what they hear in a new way, as a dawning truth, new and touching them at a deeper level. Simple the ideas may be, but they will resonate in people's hearts and feel fresh and vibrant. Thus will it be. Thus will Maitreya touch the hearts of men, appealing to them to aid themselves by aiding their brothers and sisters across the world. When men hear Him they will ponder deeply on what He says, and feel strangely moved by the oft-heard words. Their hearts will respond as hitherto they have not, and a new understanding and urgency will potentize their response.

Thus will Maitreya galvanize the peoples of the world to action and change. Those who have stood back will come forward and join the clamour for justice and sharing, freedom and peace.

Many, of course, will ignore Maitreya. Many will find His ideas abhorrent and dangerous or utopian and impossible of accomplishment. Some, more sinister and afraid, will see in Him the antichrist, the embodiment of all their fears. Some would have Him crucified forthwith had they the power. Many will sit quietly on the fence, unable to take a stand, for or against.

Those who can respond will grow in number and raise their voices for sharing and justice. They will gather round and support Him, and see Him as their leader and mentor, teacher and guide.

Thus will form a powerful mass of world public opinion, calling for change. More and more, governments will find it difficult to resist these demands of the people and will be forced to implement some degree of change.

The people will grow in power and their voices, potentized by Maitreya, will grow in strength and clarity of demand. They will call for their Spokesman to speak to the world and the stage will be set for the Day of Declaration, the first day of the New Dawn.

The Day of Declaration, on which, for the first time, Maitreya will acknowledge His true stature and name, will stand out, through history, as the turning point in the evolution of mankind. It will be inscribed in the annals as the Day of Days, the Beginning of the New, the Sanctification of Mankind, the Portal to the glorious future which awaits humanity. That day is not far off.

November 2006

THE SON OF MAN

by the Master —, through Benjamin Creme

Many people await the return of the Christ with trepidation and fear. They sense that His appearance will promote great changes in all departments of life. His values, they rightly assume, will necessarily alter their ways of thinking and living and they blanch at such a prospect. Besides, so mystical has been the view of the Christ presented down the centuries by the churches that many fear His judgement and omnipotent power; they await Him as God come to punish the wicked and reward the faithful.

It is sadly to be regretted that such a distorted vision of the Christ should so have permeated human consciousness. No such being exists. In order to understand the true nature of the Christ it is necessary to see Him as one among equal Sons of God, each endowed with full divine potential, differing only in the degree of manifestation of that divinity.

That He has achieved the fullness of that divinity is His Glory, and well may we stand in reverence at this achievement. That this same achievement is rare indeed is also indisputably true. But the wonder of the Christ for men is that He was one of them. Naught there is, in the trials and sufferings of men, but He did know it. Each step of the path that men still tread has He painfully trodden. Nothing is there, in the whole panorama of human experience, that He has not shared. Thus truly is He the Son of Man.

There can be little doubt that were He to appear unannounced in our midst few would recognize Him. So far from the general notion is He that He would pass unnoticed in the crowd. Thus it is today among His brothers as He awaits man's invitation to begin His mission. Many who see Him daily know Him not. Others recognize Him but are afraid to speak. Still others wait and pray, hopeful that He may be the One for Whom they dare not hope. Only His Declaration before the world will establish Him in the sight and hearts of men.

While we await that Day of Days, let us clarify in our minds the reasons for His return. Let us understand the nature of the task which He has set Himself. To establish in our midst the fact of God, has He come. To recreate the Divine Mysteries, is He here. To teach men how to love, and love again, is He among us. To establish man's brotherhood does He walk the Earth once more. To keep faith with the Father and with man does He accept this burden. To usher in the New Age has He returned. To consolidate the treasure of the past, to inspire the marvels of the future, to glorify God and man has He descended from His high mountain.

Let us look at His priorities: the establishment of peace; the inauguration of the system of sharing; the removal of guilt and fear — the cleansing of the hearts and minds of men; the education of mankind in the laws of life and love; an introduction to the Mysteries; the beautification of our cities; the removal of barriers to travel and interchange of peoples; the creation of a pool of knowledge accessible to all.

That such a task is not an easy one, not even for the Son of Man, is clear. Ancient habits of division and separation have strong roots, while fear and superstition cast their spell over millions of mankind. But never before, in the history of the world, has a Teacher come better equipped for His task. Maitreya has come to do battle with ignorance and fear, division and want. His weapons are spiritual understanding, knowledge and love; His shining armour is Truth Itself.

June 1984

[Readers are referred to Benjamin Creme's commentary on this article in 'Maitreya's Priorities' published in *Maitreya's Mission, Volume Three*, Chapter 1.]

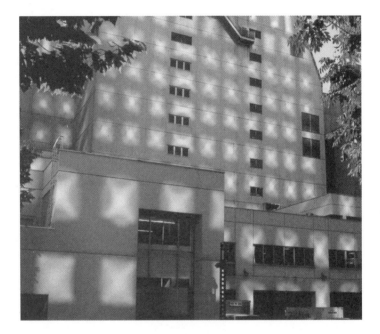

Light patterns on Tokyu Department Store in Sapporo,
Hokkaido, Japan

Light patterns on a building in the centre of
Split, Croatia (Photo: Vlatka Baksa)

The 'Hand' of Maitreya

This photograph shows the handprint of Maitreya Himself, miraculously manifested on a bathroom mirror in Barcelona, Spain in 2001. It is not a simple handprint but a three-dimensional image with photographic detail.

By placing your hand over it, or simply looking at it, Maitreya's healing and help can be invoked (subject to Karmic Law). Until Maitreya emerges fully, and we see His face, it is the closest He can come to us.

"My help is yours to command, you have only to ask."
Maitreya, the World Teacher
from Message no. 49

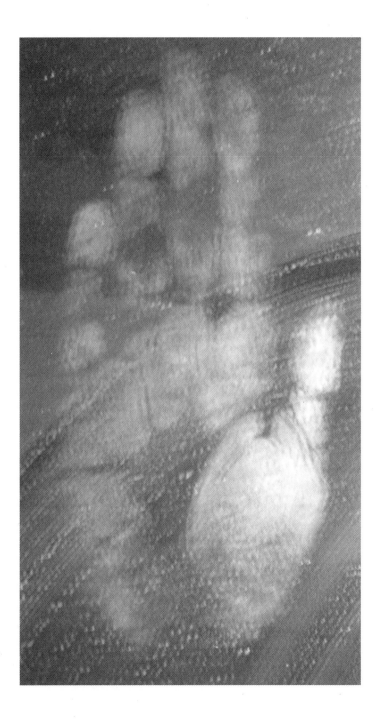

TRANSMISSION MEDITATION

A BRIEF EXPLANATION

A group meditation providing both a dynamic service to the world and powerful, personal spiritual development.

Transmission Meditation is a group meditation established to better distribute spiritual energies from their Custodians, the Masters of Wisdom, our planetary Spiritual Hierarchy. It is a means of 'stepping down' (transforming) these energies so that they become accessible and useful to the general public. It is the creation, in co-operation with the Hierarchy of Masters, of a vortex or pool of higher energy for the benefit of humanity.

In March 1974, under the direction of his Master, Benjamin Creme formed the first Transmission Meditation group in London. Today there are hundreds of such groups around the world, and new groups are forming all the time.

Transmission Meditation groups provide a link whereby Hierarchy can respond to world need. The prime motive of this work is service, but it also constitutes a powerful mode of personal growth. Many people are searching for ways in which to improve the world; this desire to serve can be strong, but difficult, in our busy lives, to fulfil. Our soul needs a means to serve, but we do not always respond to its call, and so produce disequilibrium and conflict within ourselves. Transmission Meditation provides a unique opportunity for service in a potent and fully scientific way with the minimum expenditure of one's time and energy.

Benjamin Creme holds Transmission Meditation work-shops around the world. During the meditation he is overshadowed by Maitreya, the World Teacher, which allows Maitreya to confer great spiritual nourishment on the participants. Many people are inspired to begin Transmission Meditation after attending such a workshop, and many acknowledge having received healing in the process.

[Please refer to *Transmission: A Meditation for the New Age* by Benjamin Creme, Share International Foundation]

THE GREAT INVOCATION

From the point of Light within the Mind of God
Let light stream forth into the minds of men.
Let Light descend on Earth.

From the point of Love within the Heart of God
Let love stream forth into the hearts of men.
May Christ return to Earth.

From the centre where the Will of God is known
Let purpose guide the little wills of men —
The purpose which the Masters know and serve.

From the centre which we call the race of men
Let the Plan of Love and Light work out
And may it seal the door where evil dwells.

Let Light and Love and Power
restore the Plan on Earth.

●

The Great Invocation, used by the Christ for the first time in June 1945, was released by Him to humanity to enable man himself to invoke the energies which would change our world and make possible the return of the Christ and Hierarchy. This is not the form of it used by the Christ. He uses an ancient formula, seven mystic phrases long, in an ancient sacerdotal tongue. It has been translated (by Hierarchy) into terms which we can use and understand, and, translated into many languages, is used today in every country in the world.

THE PRAYER FOR THE NEW AGE

I am the creator of the universe.
I am the father and mother of the universe.
Everything comes from me.
Everything shall return to me.
Mind, spirit and body are my temples,
For the Self to realize in them
My supreme Being and Becoming.

●

The Prayer for the New Age, given by Maitreya, the World Teacher, is a great mantram or affirmation with an invocative effect. It will be a powerful tool in the recognition by us that man and God are One, that there is no separation. The 'I' is the Divine Principle behind all creation. The Self emanates from, and is identical to, the Divine Principle.

The most effective way to use this mantram is to say or think the words with focused will, while holding the attention at the ajna centre between the eyebrows. When the mind grasps the meaning of the concepts, and simultaneously the will is brought to bear, those concepts will be activated and the mantram will work. If it is said seriously every day, there will grow inside you a realization of your true Self.

GLOSSARY OF ESOTERIC TERMS

Age — World cycle, approximately 2,500 years, determined by the relation of the Earth, Sun and constellations of the zodiac.

Ageless Wisdom — An ancient body of spiritual teaching underlying all the world's religions as well as all scientific, social and cultural achievements. First made available in writing to the general public in the late 1800s by Helena Petrovna Blavatsky and in this century by Alice A. Bailey, Helena Roerich and Benjamin Creme.

Ajna centre — The energy centre (chakra) between the eyebrows. Directing centre of the personality. Its correspondence on the physical level is the pituitary gland.

Antahkarana — An invisible channel of light forming the bridge between the physical brain and the soul, built through meditation and service.

Antichrist — Energy of the Will aspect of God, in its involutionary phase, which destroys the old forms and relationships, for example at the end of an age, to prepare the way for the building forces of the Christ Principle. Manifested in Roman times through the emperor Nero and in modern times through Hitler and six of his associates.

Age of Pisces — The stream of energy, coming into our planetary life from the constellation Pisces, has for two thousand years conditioned human experience and civilization. It was inaugurated by Jesus in Palestine and at its best produces the qualities of sensitivity and sacrifice. The age of Pisces is ending and the new age of Aquarius has begun.

Aquarius — Astronomically, the age of Aquarius, now commencing and lasting 2,350-2,500 years. Esoterically, refers to the Water Carrier, the age of Maitreya, and to the spiritual energy of Aquarius: that of synthesis and brotherhood.

Ashram — A Master's group. In the Spiritual Hierarchy there are 49 ashrams, seven major and 42 subsidiary, each headed by a Master of Wisdom.

Astral body — The emotional vehicle of an individual.

Astral plane — The plane of the emotions, including the polar opposites such as hope and fear, sentimental love and hate, happiness and suffering. The plane of illusion.

Astral Polarization — The focus of consciousness is on the astral plane. The first race, the Lemurian, had the goal of perfecting physical-plane consciousness. Atlantean man's goal was the perfecting of astral/emotional consciousness. The majority of humanity today are still polarized on the astral plane. See also Mental Polarization.

Avatar — A spiritual Being Who 'descends' in answer to mankind's call and need. There are human, planetary and cosmic Avatars. The latter would be called 'Divine Incarnations'. Their teaching, correctly apprehended and gradually applied by humanity, expands our understanding and presents the next step forward in humanity's evolutionary development.

Avatar of Synthesis — A great cosmic Being Who embodies the energies of Will, Love, Intelligence and another energy for which we have as yet no name. Since the 1940s He has been sending these energies into the world, gradually transforming division into unity.

Buddha — Last Avatar of the age of Aries. Previous World Teacher Who manifested through the Prince Gautama around 500 BC. The Embodiment of Wisdom, He currently acts as the 'Divine Intermediary' between Shamballa and Hierarchy. Buddhists expect their next great teacher under the name Maitreya Buddha.

Buddhi — The universal soul or mind; higher reason; loving understanding; love-wisdom. The energy of love as the Masters experience it.

Buddhic plane — Plane of divine intuition.

Causal body — The vehicle of expression of the soul on the causal plane. The receptacle where consciousness of one's evolutionary point of development is stored.

Causal plane — The third of the four higher mental planes on which the soul dwells.

Chakras — Energy centres (vortices) in the etheric body related to the spine and the seven most important endocrine glands. Responsible for the co-ordination and vitalization of all the bodies (mental, astral and physical) and their correlation with the soul, the main centre of consciousness. There are seven major chakras and 42 lesser ones.

Christ — A term used to designate the head of the Spiritual Hierarchy; the World Teacher; the Master of all the Masters. The office presently held by the Lord Maitreya.

Christ Consciousness — The energy of the Cosmic Christ, also known as the Christ Principle. Embodied for us by the Christ, it is at present awakening in the hearts of millions of people all over the world. The energy of evolution *per se*.

Day of Declaration — The day on which Maitreya will make Himself known to the world during a worldwide radio and television broadcast. Even those who are not listening or watching will hear His words telepathically in their own language and, at the same time, hundreds of thousands of spontaneous healings will take place throughout the world. The beginning of Maitreya's open mission in the world.

Deva — Angel or celestial being belonging to a kingdom in nature evolving parallel to humanity and ranging from subhuman elementals to superhuman beings on a level with a planetary Logos. They are the 'active builders', working intelligently with substance to create all the forms we see, including the mental, emotional and physical bodies of humanity.

Energy — From the esoteric point of view, there is nothing but energy in the whole of the manifested universe. Energy vibrates at various frequencies, and the particular frequency determines the form which the energy will take. Energy can be acted upon and directed by thought.

Esotericism — The philosophy of the evolutionary process both in man and the lower kingdoms in nature. The science of the accumulated wisdom of the ages. Presents a systematic and comprehensive account of the energetic structure of the universe and of man's place within it. Describes the forces and influences that lie behind the phenomenal world. Also, the process of becoming aware of and gradually mastering these forces.

Etheric Body — The energetic counterpart of the physical body, composed of seven major centres (chakras) and 42 minor centres; a network which connects all the centres and infinitesimally small threads of energy (nadis) which underlie every part of the nervous system. Blockages in the etheric body can result in physical illnesses.

Etheric Planes — Four planes of matter finer than the gaseous-physical, as yet invisible to most people.

Evil — Anything which impedes evolutionary development.

Evolution — The process of spiritualization of matter; the way back to the Source. The casting aside of the veils of delusion and illusion leading eventually to cosmic consciousness.

Forces of Light (Forces of Evolution) — The Spiritual Hierarchy of our planet. Planetary centre of Love-Wisdom. See also Spiritual Hierarchy.

Forces of Darkness (Forces of Evil, Forces of Materiality)
— The involutionary or materialistic forces which uphold the matter aspect of the planet. When they overstep their role and impinge upon the spiritual progress of humanity, they are designated as 'evil'.

Glamour — Illusion on the astral plane. The condition when the mind becomes veiled by emotional impulses generated on astral levels, preventing the mind's eye from clearly distinguishing reality. Examples: fear, self-pity, criticism, suspicion, self-righteousness, over-materiality.

God (see also Logos) — The great Cosmic Being Who ensouls this planet, embodying all the Laws and all the energies governed by those Laws which make up everything that we see and cannot see.

Great Invocation — An ancient formula translated by Hierarchy for the use of mankind to invoke the energies which will change our world. Translated into many languages, it is used daily by millions of people.

Guru — A spiritual teacher.

Hierarchy — See Spiritual Hierarchy.

Hierophant — The Initiator. Either the Christ, at the first two planetary initiations, or the Lord of the World, at the third and higher initiations.

Illusion — Deception on the mental plane. The soul, using the glamoured mind as its instrument, obtains a distorted picture of the phenomenal world.

Imam Mahdi — The prophet Whose return is awaited by some Islamic sects in order that He can complete the work started by Mohammed.

Incarnation — Manifestation of the soul as a threefold personality, under the Law of Rebirth.

Initiation — A voluntary process whereby successive and graded stages of unification and at-onement take place between the man or woman in incarnation, his/her soul, and the divine Monad or 'spark of God'. Each stage confers on the initiate a deeper understanding of the meaning and purpose of God's Plan, a fuller awareness of his/her part in that Plan, and an increasing ability to work consciously and intelligently towards its fulfilment.

Involution — The process whereby spirit descends into matter, its polar opposite.

Jesus — A Master of Wisdom and disciple of the Christ, Maitreya. Allowed the Christ to work through Him during the period from His baptism to the crucifixion. In the coming time, He will play a major role in reinspiring and reorienting the whole field of Christian religion. As the Master Jesus, He works closely with Maitreya, often appearing to people (in disguise).

Karma — Eastern name for the Law of Cause and Effect. The basic Law governing our existence in this solar system. Every thought we have, every action we make, sets into motion a cause. These causes have their effects, which make our lives, for good or ill. Expressed in biblical terms: "As you sow, so shall you reap."; in scientific terms: "For every action there is an equal and opposite reaction."

Krishna — A great Avatar Who appeared around 3,000 BC and served as the vehicle of manifestation for the Lord Maitreya during the age of Aries. By demonstrating the need to control the astral/emotional nature, Krishna opened the door to the second initiation. Hindus expect a new incarnation of Krishna at the end of Kali Yuga, the dark age.

Law of Cause and Effect (Law of Action and Reaction) — See Karma.

Law of Rebirth — See Reincarnation.

Logos — God. The Cosmic Being Who ensouls a planet (Planetary Logos), a solar system (Solar Logos), a galaxy (Galactic Logos) and so on to infinity.

Lord of the World — See Sanat Kumara.

Maitreya — The World Teacher for the age of Aquarius. The Christ and head of the Spiritual Hierarchy of our planet. The Master of all the Masters.

Man/Woman — The physical manifestation of a spiritual Monad (or Self), which is a single spark of the One Spirit (God).

Manas — Higher mind.

Mantram — Formula or arrangement of words or syllables which, when correctly sounded, invokes energy.

Master Djwhal Khul (D.K.) — One of the Masters of the Wisdom, known as the Tibetan, Who dictated the latest phase of the Ageless Wisdom Teaching through the disciple Alice A. Bailey. He was also responsible for the material in the books of Helena Blavatsky, *The Secret Doctrine* and *Isis Unveiled*.

Masters of Wisdom — Individuals Who have taken the fifth initiation, having passed through all the experiences that life in this world offers and, in the process, having acquired total mastery over themselves and the laws of nature. Custodians of the Plan of evolution and all the energies entering this planet which bring about the fulfilment of the Plan.

Meditation — Scientific means of contacting one's soul and of eventually becoming at one with the soul. Also the process of being open to spiritual impression and thus to co-operation with the Spiritual Hierarchy.

Mental body — The vehicle of the personality on the mental planes.

Mental plane — The plane of the mind where the mental processes take place.

Mental Polarization — The focus of consciousness on the mental plane. The shifting of consciousness on to the mental plane begins about half-way between the first and second planetary initiations.

Monad/Self — Pure Spirit reflecting the triplicity of Deity: (1) Divine Will or Power (the Father); (2) Love-Wisdom (the Son); (3) Active Intelligence (the Holy Spirit). The 'spark of God' resident in every human being.

Occult — Hidden. The hidden science of energy (see Esotericism).

Overshadowing — A voluntary co-operative process in which a Master's consciousness temporarily enters and works through the physical, emotional and mental bodies of a disciple.

Permanent atoms — The three atoms of matter — physical, astral and mental — around which the bodies for a new incarnation are formed. They retain the vibratory rate of the individual at the moment of death, guaranteeing that the energetic evolutionary 'status' thus far achieved will be carried over into successive lives.

Personality — Threefold vehicle of the soul on the physical plane, consisting of a mental, an emotional (astral) and a physical-etheric body.

Physical plane — The lowest vibrational states of substance, including: dense-physical, liquid, gaseous and etheric matter.

Plane — A level of manifestation.

Planetary Logos — Divine Being ensouling a planet.

Pralaya — A non-mental, non-astral, non-material state of existence, somewhere between death and rebirth, where the life impulse is in abeyance. An experience of perfect peace and unending bliss prior to taking the next incarnation. Corresponds to the Christian idea of paradise.

Rays — The seven streams of universal divine energy, each the expression of a great Life, Whose interaction at every conceivable frequency creates the solar systems, galaxies and universes. Movement of these energies, in spiralling cycles, draws all Being into and out of manifestation, colouring and saturating it with specific qualities and attributes.

Rays of Nations — Each nation is governed by two rays, a soul ray, which is sensed and expressed by the initiates and disciples of the nation, and a personality ray, which is the dominant mass influence and expression. From time to time, through the activities of the initiates and disciples of a country, the soul ray may be given expression and the true quality of the nation can be seen.

Reincarnation (Law of Rebirth) — The process which allows God, through an agent (ourselves) to bring Itself down to Its polar opposite — matter — in order to bring that matter back into Itself, totally imbued with the nature of God. The Law of Karma draws us back into incarnation until gradually, through the evolutionary process, we reveal more truly our innate divinity.

Sanat Kumara — The Lord of the World; the etheric-physical expression of our Planetary Logos Who dwells on Shamballa. A great Being, originally from Venus, Who sacrificed Himself to become the personality vehicle for the ensouling Deity of our planet 18.5 million years ago. The nearest aspect of God that we can know.

Self/Monad — The divine spark within every human being.

Self-realization — The process of recognizing and expressing our divine nature.

Shamballa — A centre of energy; the major centre in the

planet. It is located above the Gobi Desert on the two highest etheric planes. From it and through it flows the Shamballa Force — the energy of Will or Purpose. It corresponds to the crown centre (chakra).

Solar Logos — Divine Being ensouling our solar system.

Soul (Ego, Higher Self, inner ruler, Christ within, Son of Mind, Solar Angel) — The linking principle between Spirit and matter; between God and His form. Provides consciousness, character and quality to all manifestation in form.

Spirit — As used by Maitreya, a term meaning the sum total of all the energies — the life force — animating and vitalizing an individual. Also used, more esoterically, to mean the Monad which reflects itself in the soul.

Spirit of Peace or Equilibrium — A cosmic Being Who assists the work of Maitreya by overshadowing Him with His energy. He works closely with the Law of Action and Reaction to transform the present chaotic conditions into the opposite state in exact proportion.

Spiritual — The quality of any activity which drives the human being forward towards some form of development — physical, emotional, intuitional, social — in advance of his/her present state.

Spiritual Hierarchy (White Brotherhood, Society of Illumined Minds) — The Kingdom of God, the Spiritual Kingdom or the Kingdom of souls, made up of the Masters and initiates of all degrees and Whose purpose is to implement the Plan of God. Planetary centre of Love-Wisdom.

Three Spiritual Festivals — Determined by the full moons of Aries, Taurus and Gemini (April, May and June). These festivals, celebrated as the Easter, Wesak and Christ Festivals, will be central to the New World Religion and will constitute, each of them, a great Approach to Deity — the evocation of the Divine Light, Divine Love, and Divine Will, which can then be anchored on the Earth and utilised by man.

Transmission Meditation — A group meditation for the purpose of 'stepping down' (transforming) spiritual energies emanating from the Spiritual Hierarchy of Masters which thus become accessible and useful to the general public. It is the creation of a vortex or pool of higher energy for the benefit of humanity. This is a form of service which is simple to do, and is at the same time a powerful means of personal growth. There are hundreds of Transmission Meditation groups active in many countries around the world.

Triangle — A group of three people who link up each day in thought for a few minutes of creative meditation.

Vehicle — The form by means of which higher beings find expression on the lower planes. The physical, astral and mental bodies, for instance, form the vehicles of the soul on lower levels.

Vibration — Movement of energy. All energy vibrates at its own particular frequency. The evolutionary process proceeds through a heightening of the vibrational rate in response to higher incoming energies.

World Teacher — The head of the Spiritual Hierarchy in any given cycle. The Master of all the Masters. The office held at present by the Lord Maitreya.

Yoga — Union of the lower nature with the higher. Also, different forms and techniques to gain control of the physical, astral or mental bodies.

BOOKS BY BENJAMIN CREME

(Listed in order of publication)

The Reappearance of the Christ and the Masters of Wisdom

In his first book, Benjamin Creme gives the background and pertinent information concerning the emergence of Maitreya (the Christ), as World Teacher for the New Age now dawning. Expected under different names by all religious groups, Maitreya comes to help us create co-operation among the many ideological factions, galvanize world goodwill and sharing, and inspire sweeping political, social, economic and environmental reforms. Benjamin Creme puts the most profound event of the last 2,000 years into its correct historical and esoteric context and describes what effect the World Teacher's presence will have on both the world's institutions and the average person. Through his telepathic contact with a Master of Wisdom, Creme offers insights on such subjects as: the soul and reincarnation, fear of death, telepathy, meditation, nuclear energy, ancient civilizations, UFOs, problems of the developing world, a new economic order, the antichrist, and the 'Last Judgement'.

1st edition 1979. 2nd edition 2007. ISBN: 978-90-71484-32-2, 288pp.

Messages from Maitreya the Christ

During the years of preparation for His emergence, Maitreya gave 140 Messages through Benjamin Creme during public lectures in London from 1977 to 1982. The method used was mental overshadowing and a telepathic rapport thus set up.

Maitreya's Messages of sharing, co-operation and unity inspire readers to spread the news of His reappearance and to work urgently for the rescue of millions suffering from poverty and starvation in a world of plenty. In Message No. 11 Maitreya says: "My Plan is to show you that the way out of your problems is to listen again to the true voice of God within your hearts, to share the produce of this most bountiful of worlds among your brothers and sisters everywhere. . . ."

Maitreya's words are a unique source of wisdom, hope and succour at this critical time of world change, and when read aloud these profound yet simple Messages invoke His energy and blessing.

1st edition Vol. I 1981, Vol. II 1986. 2nd, combined, edition 1992, reprinted 2001. ISBN 978-90-71484-22-3, 286pp.

Transmission: A Meditation for the New Age

Transmission Meditation is a form of group meditation for the purpose of 'stepping down' (transforming) spiritual energies which thus become accessible and useful to the general public. It is the creation, in co-operation with the Hierarchy of Masters, of a vortex or pool of higher energy for the benefit of humanity.

Introduced in 1974 by Benjamin Creme, under the direction of his Master, this is a form of service which is simple to do and is at the same time a powerful means of personal growth. The meditation is a combination of two yogas: Karma Yoga (yoga of service) and Laya Yoga (yoga of energy or chakras). It is a service in which we can be involved for the rest of our lives knowing that we are helping the evolution of humanity into, and beyond, the New Age. There are hundreds of Transmission Meditation groups active in many countries around the world.

In this practical and inspiring book, Benjamin Creme describes the aims, technique and results of Transmission Meditation, as well as the underlying purpose of the meditation for the development of disciples.

1st edition 1983. 5th edition 2006. ISBN 978-90-71484-35-3, 212 pp.

A Master Speaks

Humanity is guided from behind the scenes by a highly evolved and illumined group of men Who have preceded us along the path of evolution. These Masters of Wisdom, as They are called, seldom appear openly, but usually work through Their disciples – men and women who influence society through their work in science, education, art, religion, politics, and in every department of life.

British artist Benjamin Creme is a disciple of a Master with Whom he is in close telepathic contact. Since the launching of *Share International*, the magazine of which Benjamin Creme is editor, his Master has contributed to every issue an inspiring article on a wide range of subjects: reason and intuition, the new civilization, health and healing, the art of living, the need for synthesis, justice is divine, the Son of Man, human rights, the law of rebirth, the end of hunger, sharing for peace, the rise of people power, the brightest future, co-operation – and many more.

The major purpose of these articles is to draw attention to the needs of the present and the immediate future time, and to give information about the teachings of Maitreya, the Master of all the Masters. This third edition contains all 223 articles from the first 22 volumes of *Share International*.

1st edition 1985. 3rd expanded edition 2004.
ISBN 978-90-71484-29-2, 452pp.

Maitreya's Mission, Volume One

The first of a trilogy of books which describe the emergence and teachings of Maitreya, the World Teacher. As human consciousness steadily matures, many of the ancient 'mysteries' are now being revealed. This volume can be seen as a guidebook for humanity as it travels on the evolutionary journey. The book's canvas is vast: from the new teachings of the Christ to meditation and karma, from life after death and reincarnation to healing and social transformation, from initiation and the role of service to the Seven Rays, from Leonardo da Vinci and Mozart to Sathya Sai Baba. It sets the scene and prepares the way for the work of Maitreya, as World Teacher, and the creation of a new and better life for all. It is a powerful message of hope.

1st edition 1986. 3rd edition 1993, reprinted 2003. ISBN 978-90-71484-08-7, 419pp.

Maitreya's Mission, Volume Two

This inspiring and heart-warming book offers new hope and guidance to a suffering world on the threshold of a Golden Age. It presents the teachings of Maitreya, the World Teacher, on both the outer, practical, and inner, spiritual levels; His uniquely accurate forecasts of world events, which have astonished international media; and His miraculous appearances which have brought hope and inspiration to many thousands. It also contains a series of unique interviews with Benjamin Creme's Master which throw new and revealing light on some of the greatest problems facing humanity.

This book covers an enormous range: Maitreya's teachings, the growth of consciousness, new forms of government, commercialization and market forces, the Principle of Sharing, life in the New Age, schools without walls, the Technology of Light, crop circles, the Self, telepathy, disease and death, energy and thought, Transmission Meditation, the soul's purpose. Also includes transcripts of Benjamin Creme's inspiring talks on 'The Overcoming of Fear' and 'The Call to Service'.

1st edition 1993, reprinted 2004. ISBN 978-90-71484-11-7, 753pp.

The Ageless Wisdom Teaching

An overview of humanity's spiritual legacy, this book serves as a concise and easy-to-understand introduction to the Ageless Wisdom Teaching. It explains the basic tenets of esotericism, including: source of the Teaching, the emergence of the World Teacher, rebirth and reincarnation, the Law of Cause and Effect, the Plan of evolution, origin of man, meditation and service, future changes. Also included is an esoteric glossary and a recommended reading list.

1st edition 1996, reprinted 2006. ISBN 978-90-71484-13-1, 76pp

Maitreya's Mission, Volume Three

Benjamin Creme presents a compelling vision of the future. With Maitreya, the World Teacher, and His disciples, the Masters of Wisdom, openly offering Their guidance, humanity will create a civilization worthy of its divine potential. Peace will be established; sharing the world's resources the norm; maintaining our environment a top priority. The new education will teach the fact of the soul and the evolution of consciousness. The cities of the world will be transformed into centres of great beauty.

This book offers invaluable wisdom on a vast range of topics. It includes Maitreya's priorities for the future, and an interview with a Master of Wisdom on 'The Challenge of the 21st Century'. It explores karma and reincarnation, the origin of humanity, meditation and service, the Plan of evolution, and other fundamental concepts of the Ageless Wisdom Teachings. It includes a fascinating look, from an esoteric, spiritual perspective, at 10 famous artists – among them Leonardo da Vinci, Michelangelo and Rembrandt – by Benjamin Creme, himself an artist.

Like the first two volumes of *Maitreya's Mission*, this work combines profound spiritual truths with practical solutions to today's most vexing problems. It is indeed a message of hope for a humanity ready to "begin the creation of a civilization such as this world has never yet seen".

1st edition 1997. ISBN 978-90-71484-15-5, 705pp.

The Great Approach: New Light and Life for Humanity

This prophetic book addresses the problems of our chaotic world and its gradual change under the influence of a group of perfected men, the Masters of Wisdom, Who, with Their leader Maitreya, the World Teacher, are returning openly to the world for the first time in 98,000 years.

The book covers such topics as: sharing, the USA in a quandary; ethnic conflicts, crime and violence, environment and pollution, genetic engineering, science and religion, the nature of light, health and healing, education, miracles, the soul and incarnation. An extraordinary synthesis of knowledge, it throws a searchlight on the future; with clear vision it predicts our highest achievements of thought to reveal the amazing scientific discoveries which lie ahead. It shows us a world in which war is a thing of the past, and the needs of all are met.

1st edition 2001. ISBN 978-90-71484-23-0, 320pp.

The Art of Co-operation

The Art of Co-operation deals with the most pressing problems of our time, and their solution, from the point of view of the Ageless Wisdom Teachings that, for millennia, have revealed the forces underlying the outer world. Benjamin Creme brings these teachings up to date, preparing the way for the imminent emergence of Maitreya, the World Teacher, and His group of Masters of Wisdom.

This volume looks at a world locked in ancient competition, trying to solve its problems by old and out-worn methods, while the answer – co-operation – lies in our own hands. It shows the way to a world of justice, freedom and peace through a growing appreciation of the unity underlying all life. Maitreya will inspire in us this growing realization.

Topics include: the necessity of co-operation, the USA and competition, organism versus organization, opportunity for service, fear of loss, karma, love, courage and detachment, overcoming of glamour, how the Masters teach, unity in diversity, consensus, trust.

1st edition 2002. ISBN 978-90-71484-26-1, 235pp.

Maitreya's Teachings: The Laws of Life

We do not have even fragments of the teachings of former World Teachers given prior to certain knowledge of Their existence. We do not have the teachings of a Christ, or a Buddha, or a Krishna, except as seen through the eyes of later followers. For the first time we are given the flavour of the thoughts and insights of a Being of immeasurable stature to enable us to understand the path of evolution stretching ahead of us which He has come to outline for us. The impression left in the mind by the Teacher is that the breadth and depth of His knowledge and awareness have no limits; that He is tolerant and wise beyond conception, and of amazing humility.

Few could read from these pages without being changed. To some the extraordinary insights into world events will be of major interest, while to others the laying bare of the secrets of Self-realization, the simple description of experienced truth, will be a revelation. To anyone seeking to understand the Laws of Life, these subtle and pregnant insights will take them quickly to the core of Life itself, and provide them with a simple path stretching to the mountain-top. The essential unity of all life is underscored in a clear and meaningful way. Never, it would appear, have the Laws by which we live seemed so natural and so unconstraining.

1st edition, 2005. ISBN 978-90-71484-31-5, 258pp.

The Art of Living: Living Within the Laws of Life

Inspired by the writings of two Masters of Wisdom – the Master Djwhal Khul and, particularly, Benjamin Creme's own Master – Part One of this book considers the experience of living as a form of art, like painting or music. To reach a high level of expression requires both knowledge of and adherence to certain fundamental principles. In the art of life, it is through the understanding of the great Law of Cause and Effect, and the related Law of Rebirth, that we achieve the poised harmlessness that leads to personal happiness, right human relations and the correct path for all humanity on its evolutionary journey.

Parts Two and Three, 'The Pairs of Opposites' and 'Illusion', propose that it is man's unique position in the evolutionary scheme – the meeting point of spirit and matter – that produces his seemingly endless struggle both within himself and in outer living. The means by which he emerges from the fog of illusion, and blends these two aspects of himself into one perfect Whole, is living life itself with growing detachment and objective self-awareness.

1st edition 2006. ISBN 978- 90-71484-37-7, 215pp.

The World Teacher for All Humanity

Maitreya, the World Teacher, stands poised, ready to emerge into full public work. This book presents an overview of this momentous event: the return to the everyday world of Maitreya in July 1977 and the gradual emergence of His group, the Masters of Wisdom; the enormous changes that Maitreya's presence has brought about; and His plans, priorities and recommendations for the immediate future. It discusses in detail the quality and capacity of Maitreya based on a series of articles written by Benjamin Creme's Master – Maitreya as a great spiritual Avatar with immeasurable love, wisdom and power; and, as a friend and brother of humanity who is here to lead the whole of humanity into the New Age of Aquarius.

1st edition, 2007. ISBN 978-90-71484-39-1, 132pp.

~~~

These books are published by Share International Foundation (Amsterdam, London). Most have been translated and published in Dutch, French, German, Japanese and Spanish by groups responding to this message. Some have also been published in Chinese, Croatian, Finnish, Greek, Hebrew, Italian, Portuguese, Romanian, Russian, Slovenian and Swedish. Further translations are planned.

Books are available from local booksellers as well as online vendors.

SHARE INTERNATIONAL

A unique magazine featuring each month: up-to-date information about the emergence of Maitreya, the World Teacher; an article from a Master of Wisdom; expansions of the esoteric teachings; Benjamin Creme's answers to a wide variety of topical and esoteric questions; articles by and interviews with people at the forefront of progressive world change; news from UN agencies and reports of positive developments in the transformation of our world.

Share International brings together the two major directions of New Age thinking — the political and the spiritual. It shows the synthesis underlying the political, social, economic and spiritual changes now occurring on a global scale, and seeks to stimulate practical action to rebuild our world along more just and compassionate lines.

Share International covers news, events and comments related to Maitreya's priorities: an adequate supply of the right food, housing and shelter for all, healthcare and education as universal rights, and the maintenance of ecological balance in the world.

ISSN 0169-1341

Versions of *Share International* are available in Dutch, French, German, Japanese, Romanian, Slovenian and Spanish. For subscription information, contact the appropriate office below.

For North, Central and South America,
Australia, New Zealand and the Philippines
Share International
PO Box 971, North Hollywood, CA 91603, USA

For the UK
Share International
PO Box 3677, London NW5 1RU, UK

For the rest of the world
Share International
PO Box 41877, 1009 DB Amsterdam, Holland

Extensive information and excerpts from the magazine are published online at: **www.share-international.org**

ABOUT THE AUTHOR

Scottish-born painter and esotericist Benjamin Creme has for over 30 years been preparing the world for the most extraordinary event in human history — the return of our spiritual mentors to the everyday world.

Benjamin Creme has appeared on television, radio and in documentary films worldwide and lectures throughout Western and Eastern Europe, the USA, Japan, Australia, New Zealand, Canada and Mexico.

Trained and supervised over many years by his own Master, he began his public work in 1974. In 1982 he announced that the Lord Maitreya, the long-awaited World Teacher, was living in London, ready to present Himself openly when invited by the media to do so. This event is now imminent.

Benjamin Creme continues to carry out his task as messenger of this inspiring news. His books, fourteen at present, have been translated into many languages. He is also the editor of *Share International* magazine, which circulates in over 70 countries. He accepts no money for any of this work.

Benjamin Creme lives in London, is married, and has three children.